Y0-CUZ-267

DAILY
Guideposts
JOURNAL
2006

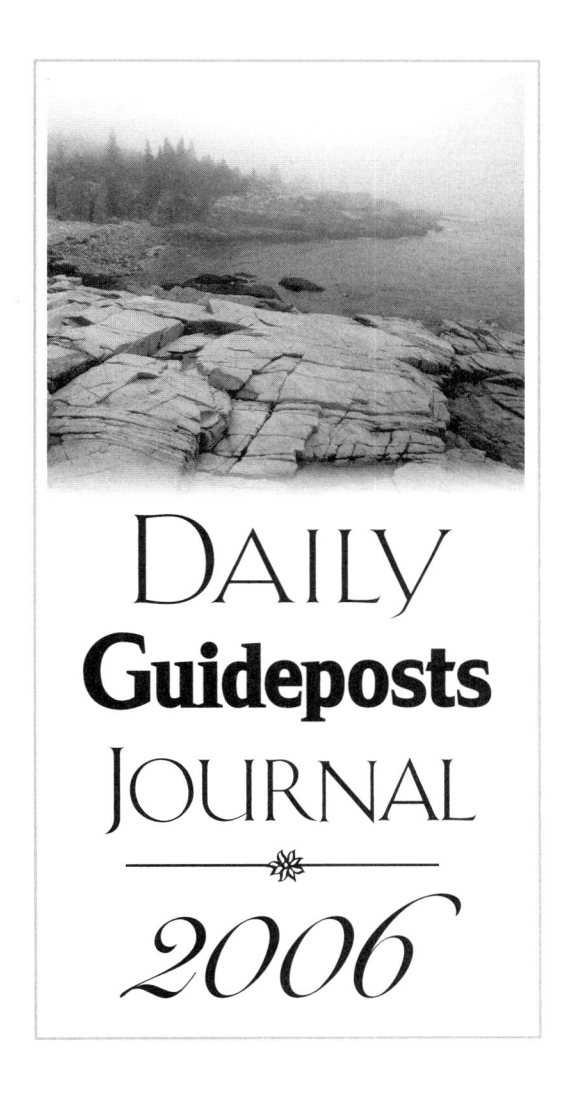

IDEALS PUBLICATIONS
A DIVISION OF GUIDEPOSTS
NASHVILLE, TENNESSEE

ISBN 0-8249-4644-8

Published by Ideals Publications
A division of Guideposts
535 Metroplex Drive, Suite 250
Nashville, Tennessee 37211
www.idealsbooks.com

Copyright © 2005 by Ideals Publications

All rights reserved. No part of this publication may be reproduced or transmitted
in any form or by any means, electronic or mechanical, including photocopy, recording,
or any information storage and retrieval system, without permission in writing from the publisher.

Publisher, Patricia A. Pingry
Editor, Peggy Schaefer
Designer, Marisa Calvin
Copy Editor, Melinda Rathjen
Cover photograph © by David Sanger Photography/Alamy

Printed and bound in the United States of America
10 9 8 7 6 5 4 3 2 1

ACKNOWLEDGMENTS

All Scripture quotations, unless otherwise noted, are taken from *The King James Version of the Bible*.

Scripture quotations marked (AMP) are taken from *The Amplified Bible*, © 1965 by Zondervan Publishing House. All rights reserved.

Scripture quotations marked (JB) are taken from *The Jerusalem Bible*, © 1966, 1967, and 1968 by Darton, Longman & Todd Ltd. and Doubleday & Company, Inc. All rights reserved.

Scripture quotations marked (MSG) are taken from *The Message*. Copyright © 1993, 1994, 1995, 1996, 2000, 2001, 2002 by Eugene H. Peterson.

Scripture quotations marked (NAS) are taken from the *New American Standard Bible*, © The Lockman Foundation, 1960, 1962, 1963, 1968, 1971, 1972, 1973, 1975, 1977. Used by permission.

Scripture quotations marked (NEB) are taken from *The New English Bible*. Copyright © The Delegates of the Oxford University Press and the Syndics of the Cambridge University Press 1961, 1970.

Scripture quotations marked (NIV) are taken from *The Holy Bible, New International Version*. Copyright © 1973, 1978, 1984 International Bible Society. Used by permission of Zondervan Bible Publishers.

Scripture quotations marked (NKJV) are taken from *The Holy Bible, New King James Version*. Copyright © 1997, 1990, 1985, 1983 by Thomas Nelson, Inc.

Scripture quotations marked (NLT) are taken from the *Holy Bible*, New Living Translation. Copyright © 1996. Used by permission of Tyndale House Publishers, Inc., Wheaton, Illinois 60189. All rights reserved.

Scripture quotations marked (NRSV) are taken from the *New Revised Standard Version Bible*. Copyright © 1989 by the Division of Christian Education of the National Council of the Churches of Christ in the U.S.A. Used by permission. All rights reserved.

Scripture quotations marked (RSV) are taken from the *Revised Standard Version of the Bible*. Copyright © 1946, 1952, 1971 by Division of Christian Education of the National Council of Churches of Christ in the U.S.A. Used by permission.

Scripture quotations marked (TLB) are taken from *The Living Bible*. Copyright © 1971 by Tyndale House Publishers, Wheaton, IL 60187. All rights reserved.

Introduction

A journal can be an invaluable tool for your faith-building journey. It provides a space in which to set goals, examine questions, reflect upon experiences, and offer up praise and thanksgiving for your blessings. As a written record of your daily thoughts, *Daily Guideposts Journal 2006* will allow you to look back at the end of the year and see the progress you have made. Have you deepened your faith and become closer to God? Have you become more like the person you want to be? Have your prayers been answered and your dreams fulfilled? By reading through your past entries, you will know with surety the answers to these questions, as well as the areas of your life that most need your focus.

In *Daily Guideposts Journal 2006*, each day of the year receives its own page and features a Bible verse and a question or prayer to get you started on your writing for that day. These features are included to help you explore your faith and your relationship with God in ways that you may not have considered before. By taking just a few minutes each day to reflect and record your thoughts, you will be able to strengthen your faith and expand your awareness of the countless ways in which God is present in your life.

The Bible verses within are drawn directly from the pages of *Daily Guideposts 2006*. They relate to both the devotions contained within *Daily Guideposts 2006* and to the questions and prayers contained within the pages of the journal. If you're a *Daily Guideposts* reader, use this journal to expand and enrich your daily practice. If you're new to *Daily Guideposts*, perhaps this journal will prompt you to reach for *Daily Guideposts* as well. There you will find devotions that inspire, comfort, encourage, motivate, and praise. There you will hear from people like yourself as they discover God in the course of their daily lives.

Spend the coming year with *Daily Guideposts Journal 2006*, celebrating God's presence in your life and rejoicing in the hope that your faith provides.

January 1

The apostles said to the Lord, "Increase our faith!" —Luke 17:5 (NIV)

What small steps can I take each day to grow my faith this year?

Up @ 7:40 - Devo - Juice - Coffee - Start Puzzle 'Happy ewe near' To 1st Evan. for technical sermon w/ Mark & Margie - Home to cereal lunch & fined puzzle - Get short nap & work out horse - Some solitude -- Help Ann a bit in kitchen - Kids arrive with Josie & Dana - Fancy dinner - See some Johnny Cash show - & football - Britt ceiling - Pork tenders - Grits - Ice cream & fancy cake - which Ann got at Sunday with me after church. Some prayer - Cleanliness - See Crossing Jordan. & news -

And I John saw the holy city, new Jerusalem, coming down from God out of heaven, prepared as a bride adorned for her husband.
—REVELATION 21:2

JANUARY 2

LORD, HELP ME TO REMEMBER THAT YOU ALONE KNOW THE PLAN FOR MY LIFE.

Devo - cm. Purell lift
Walk with Ann & Margie weights
Sports start @ 10:00
Fla. wins over Iowa - 'Bama wins last second field goal -
Notre Dame beaten by Ohio State - Big Quarterback the difference
Va. leading Georgia making comeback -
Auburn - loses? -
Texas comes to Memphis & wins by 9 points - Too many 'young' mistakes
- - Mark over for left-overs
See Sue Thomas & Early Edition - Lawyer murders brother - a death row inmate acquitted - (Tries to run jury & Reporter down in Lincoln - 3 murders already in New Year -
Win rubber in softball -

JANUARY 3

For where your treasure is, there will your heart be also. —Matthew 6:21

DO I RECOGNIZE SPIRITUAL TREASURES IN MY LIFE?

Devo + Comm puzzle. Walk with Ann & Margie. Get to see & pet Abbey. She was excited & thrilled – Call bank & take $35,000 in checks to 1st TN – on Kelly's debt. Cereal brunch then to Kroger for flowers. + Get money from Legg Mason + deposit at crescent center branch. Home to see G. Tech play Vandy – Ken & Betty take us to dinner – nice evening – play with waitress – Get pecan ball for dessert present. Home to see Sam & Them Stab & Fla. State Orange Bowl – Some of Cal Thomas & Early Edition – Some 48'ers. + Law & Order – Flowers left in car hate note.

My lover is mine and I am his; he browses among the lilies. —SONG OF SOLOMON 2:16 (NIV)

JANUARY 4

IN WHAT SPECIAL WAY CAN I CELEBRATE MY RELATIONSHIP WITH A LOVED ONE?

Birthday!
- Devo - Commercial puzzle
Computer still out -
Go to exercise - Then to Ike's - insurance - medicare not approved - Home to nap —— Mark & Marge over for dinner - see Sue Thomas - catch terrorists - save bomb blast - Get big brother - See Early Edition parts - saves woman from jumping + cons Con Man - His mom + friends get money back - His blind girlfriend - helps - shoots him with blanks - (Later off on Scam movie - Redford/Newman See best football game of all time - Rose Bowl Texas beats S. Cal in last 26 seconds Black quarterback - Best ever performance - Runs for 200. Passes for 200 - Win by 3 after 2 pt conversion - terrif!

January 5

The stranger that dwelleth with you shall be unto you as one born among you, and thou shalt love him as thyself. . . . —Leviticus 19:34

WHAT OPPORTUNITY CAN I TAKE TO ENRICH A STRANGER'S LIFE WITH KINDNESS?

Devo - commercial Russle walked 30 min. - listen & Mark - Ann to 2nd Pres. Bible Study - Check bank for account info - Checks clear for Kelly - $60,000 in bank -- Credit card payment -- Blow some leaves after un-knotting wire - Go to Brett's 5 o'clock game in which he stars - offense & defense - Rebounds - real feel for the game - Home to stir-fry & Rice - pineapple + Applesauce -- Mark comes to see Early Edition after eating out with Kelly family + Jeremy + Sorrels - & Nick --
See gang-related without a Trace - news - Willie talks - no trees to come down in Collierville. TV anti-religious series coming out.. No show in Arlington.

> "Bring my sons from afar and my daughters from the end of the earth, every one who is called by my name, whom I created for my glory, whom I formed and made." —ISAIAH 43:6–7 (RSV)

JANUARY 6

HOW IS GOD TRANSFORMING ME IN HIS LIKENESS?

Devo. — Puzzle — called Mike. Ann goes to St. Francis & sees Patty and Danielle friend — takes gift to Patty — Mike over to do leaves — They get picked up today! — Jim Wilson will come Monday to put in Dishwasher. Mary calls Ann .. she's doing fine — Call from Mary Jo. Go to Drug store & get drugs discounted thru Humana — Thanks to Barbara — Go to Mall & see Susan who says they don't want me in their store — Got Aveda B.D. present. Work puzzle with Ann — walk in house & left weights — same supper as last night… see some Atlantis search — godfathers — Close to home — Numbers & some Monk repeat — Stabbed off-duty deputy will recover — some miracles —

JANUARY 7

The God of all comfort, who comforts us in all our troubles. . . . —II Corinthians 1:3–4 (NIV)

HOW AM I REMINDED EACH DAY OF GOD'S COMFORTING PRESENCE?

Devo - Ruzelo -
Aunt Sant & grocery -
I walk inside & listen
to Bible & Music -

Watch KY get humiliated at Kansas
Go to Katherine Lucas Ball coronation
@ Lindenwood - Mark, Krista, Jeremy
Nancy & Kelly there — see old friends
who were glad to see me — Cleary - Sub SS.
classes - Katherine & Mary Ann Lucas - Elaine
Coppard - Cleonine Young - Burks, Brian
& pretty blond wife — Sharon Hodger
Rebecca - Clay shakes hand —

Home to solitaire & ball games
- Ol Miss beats Alabama - Miss State beats
Ark. Fla. beats Ga. —

New England & Redskins win
Football - See Van Dyke Mystery.
Dead hubby isn't dead —

The Lord is in his holy temple: let all the earth keep silence before him. —Habakkuk 2:20

JANUARY 8

HOW MIGHT I FIND A SILENT MOMENT IN WHICH TO WORSHIP THE LORD?

Devo - Puzzle - To 1st Evan. ~~former~~ Preacher Stevens - now in Bulgaria, preached - Home to lift. weights - walk - Listen to Music - short nap - prepared grill for steak supper - Mark comes late but helps - Al + Ruth come by - but won't stay for dinner - see some pro futball & some Ga. Tech\Boston B.B. - all kids show up for supper - Great dinner - B.D. presents from everyone -- Mikey gets leaf rake - (for Brilt & me) See Crossing Jordan - & news -

January 9

She seeketh wool, and flax, and worketh willingly with her hands. —Proverbs 31:13

LORD, HELP ME TO FIND WAYS THAT I CAN USE MY TALENTS FOR THE BENEFIT OF YOUR CHILDREN.

Devo - Puzzle -
Jim Wilson comes and puts in Dishwasher - hard work Go to lunch @ Cockeyed Camel with Cel + Ruth Good meal - good waitess - Home with Ruth - who hears my gum cracking - Fish Tank man comes with nurse student - I blow leaves in back Cel comes + gets maps - we hear his squirrel story - Solitaire robbers + news See Raymond after work news - Betty calls + reminds me there are two brooms - Ann finds wrench Jim needs.

Eat steak left-overs - Britt loses game we miss - See ½ See Thomas + Early Edition - stops a girl suit attempts + saves boy with help of stripper. See CSI - sister saved by drug low count - Murder in the news -

Feed me with food convenient for me.
—Proverbs 30:8

JANUARY 10

What challenge in my life do I need to turn over to God?

Devo — & Pizza — Ann to Church all A.m. — I go to W.H. Oats — Jitstore for bird food — Home Depot + hair cut — win some Hubbles — go to Butler's with Ann who brings me home — then goes back for ever — blocked in by Al's car Al propositioned by wheelchair patient at hospital — See some Raymond — lift weights + walk some — eat bean soup. Mark over for food & Sue Thomas its eye— bio attack stopped by naming small planes. Ky loses to Vandy @ Home — 15th time in 21 games. Morris back + made a difference — could have tied by 3 pt goal barely misses — Heavy rain today — — lebra off car — Got wet leaving Home Depot.

January 11

Now to the King eternal, immortal, invisible, the only God, be honor and glory forever and ever.
—I Timothy 1:17 (NAS)

When have I allowed my ego to overshadow my faith in God?

Devo - Puzzle.
Worked in house - went to P. office for stamps - woman healing may puts on a show. Women respond. To Drug store - long wait there - get Throat spray for Ann. Give candy - see Linda Guthrie + Marcia + Blaine - give candy - Read Christian guide through - solitaire - News - Raymond - Bacon & Eggs supper - Sue Thomas + First Edition - Blaine girlfriend learns of his work C31 after potter + serial news.
Marcie shows up late - Steady & charge Norelco. Call Margie - Mark may be getting sick. Bait two traps.

I trust in the mercy of God for ever and ever.
—Psalm 52:8

January 12

When am I grateful for God's mercy? Devo — + Puzzle - Lift Weights - walk for 25 minutes. Ann home from all - A.M. chestnut and Pres - we go to 1st Sven. for lunch service - Solitude - naps - back closet. Ann & I w/c/m g mall vac. - Check yard trap - see news + chan 10 news on Celito + Bush's visit to Gulf coast - - Mark & Maggie over - I go to KFC + get cheap dinners - 3 for $10 - see Sue Thomas - catch reporter murders - news man arrested - see Early Edition - Cub pitcher signs when lady TV. admits she loves him - Without a trace - Prostitutes .. fake death - to get back to her daughter - who quits - - Sure news - gas leaks -

January 13

> "Lord, let our eyes be opened."
> —Matthew 20:33 (RSV)

In what ways can my creativity reflect my spiritual values?

Devo - & Puzzles
Ann goes to store & shops @ Macy's - Buys Pajamas.
I go to Stern's & give blood. Give candy & both to girls - Rains most of morning - Read from Flip the Switch. Cereal twice -- Puzzle with Ann - some solitaire - Go to Brett's 6 o'clock game. They lose to better team but he is outstanding. Rebounds - passes - drives for reverse lay-up hit 3 3 pts. Home to some of Bye Bye Birdie Van Dyke - Ann Margaret & Janet Leigh - See some Close to Home & Numbers - More violence in News.

> "Martha, Martha," the Lord answered, "you are worried and upset about many things, but only one thing is needed. Mary has chosen what is better. . . ." —LUKE 10:41–42 (NIV)

JANUARY 14

DO I KNOW WHEN TO LET GO OF THE TASKS OF THE DAY?

Deed - & Puzzle -
Ann to Sam's with Kelly -
To spoken also -
First we work with Margie
Mark over to join me in watching Alabama beat us at home - we just don't have it! - Ole Miss beats Miss. State.
Villanova beaten by Texas
Washington sleeps -
See Denver knock out New England - No 2nd Super Bowl for them. Game was close until interception & then punt fumble locks 'em away - Ann gets on internet & gets 3 puzzles for me - & I work - but can't get Lincoln's quote " He can compress more words into a small idea than any many I know - (Webster?) Lift Weight -

JANUARY 15 23

I call to remembrance my song in the night: I commune with mine own heart. . . .
—Psalm 77:6

DO I NOTICE SIGNS OF GOD'S FAITHFULNESS WHEN THEY OCCUR?

To Surgery - at 6:30 — Got into operating room around 2:00 pm — 2 hr surgery for Pace Maker/Defibrulator — Served two meals — Mark, Kelly & Mcgregor come visit — Drugged with Celebrex — Tallia & Wendy nurse me — Watch last part of 24 hrs...

"He moves mountains without their knowing it...." —Job 9:5 (NIV)

JANUARY 16
24

DO I RECOGNIZE THE OPPORTUNITIES HIDDEN IN OBSTACLES?

Fight to get out of hospital - Deidra forgets to call - I get taxi when I call her. - Pace maker test - take medicine there I.V. for infection - Go to Stern for possible electro cardiagram - Ann takes care of me - can't raise left arm to head - can't drive for 10 days - must avoid electro-magnet & car engines - Sophie's come by with meats for supper - Ken painting in old shoes & outfit - - lie in bed @ home. Ann heats itching arm pit - See Peters & 1st Even Turner in exit lobby - Hear about Roy's taunting Ryan while he preaches - Must over for 6:00 Ky/Auburn game - Closer than should be - N. Crawford carries us Many turnovers - Young Auburn team. See Early Edition - "Cop" Rival! becomes hero - Thanks to Gary - Give up TV - head for bed.

JANUARY 17

This is the day the Lord has made; let us rejoice and be glad in it. —Psalm 118:24 (NIV)

How can I be mindful that each day is a precious gift?

Devo - Funnies - Look over programs -- Start puzzle - Bath & to Church - Mary & Mark there. Home to stretch & see Pitt - beat Manning Colts - Then Carolina over Bears - Roast Beef supper of which I ate little - no desert. See 24 hours and - last of sheriff story & chief killing killer & then getting caught -- Tells divorced wife & daughter -- shacks up - she leaves - Ambulance wrecks -
Katrina victims of Black Christian Church -

JANUARY 18

A man that hath friends must shew himself friendly: and there is a friend that sticketh closer than a brother. —Proverbs 18:24

WHAT STEPS CAN I TAKE TO BECOME A BETTER FRIEND TO OTHERS?

Devo - Puzzle - after walking in Mall with Ann & Margie. Lift weights - some stretching - some weight loss reading - see ½ of Comancheros with Stewart Whitman & John Wayne - 2 cereal meals -- Left-over dinner - & double 24 hours and Sue Thomas & Early Edition - CSI - Judge lets killer walk because he doesn't like Horatio - Margie & Mark for Supper Ann to Circle Small group at Lyn's Home. Have radio on - solitaire rebber - Buy Girl Scout Cookies from door-door 2 little girls and Mom -

JANUARY 19

The blessing of the Lord makes rich, and he adds no sorrow with it. —Proverbs 10:22 (RSV)

WHAT EXAMPLE OF GRACE MIGHT I PASS ALONG TO OTHERS?

Devo - Stretch - Get flowers at Kirby-Kroger for girls at S'rem where I see Johnson - Will have pace maker set soon - next Monday - To see Mary Wilson at Baptist - Ann Cad already come & left Camellias - Home to Cereal - Stretch - Go to Wild Oats for food & Ole's for medicine - Home to News @ 5 - some solitaire - & some Raymond. Eat hamburger early - Mask over & stay to see Ky. beat Ga. on road - Sparks & Rondo come alive --- see Sue Thomas & kidnapped deaf girl - held for Ransom. Some Early Edition - saves woman from Bod. case & two kids in boat - from carbon mon - which unites families - Louisville beaten by St. Johns - Indiana beats Illini - Corvette missing 40 years - recovered - feel better

People who want to get rich fall into temptation and a trap and into many foolish and harmful desires.... —1 Timothy 6:9 (NIV)

January 20

Is there a temptation that I need God's help to overcome?

Devo - off to exercise - To Kroger + home - Dump water off pool - work 2 puzzles + fall asleep woke when Mrs. Morton's niece? calls with Ann's phone - Do stretches - take Rejuvamen - Work puzzle with Ann - Early dinner pork + snitzel - peas - water - See some of Duke - NC State - Then Memphis win over TN. --
Sue some Sue Thomas + Early Edition. - Gary wants to die but Ghosts reminds him of the lives he's saved. @51 N.y. - Ecstasy drug runner - 2 dead models + Female Dr. shot by dying men's wife. - Fed. judge stops senate from denying @Julie Ford her seat - temporarily

JANUARY 21

Turn, O Lord, save my life; deliver me for the sake of thy steadfast love. —Psalm 6:4 (RSV)

How can I thank God for His unfailing love?

Puzzles - Devo - Stretch - Am by before I go to 1st Evcer. & sit with Patty + Bubber - meet her 2 daughters - Help her to van - Home to cereal lunch + pump pool cover - Little solitaire + read from "Flip Switch" - See some news + off to Brith's game. He plays well but not entire game - 4 fouls - Home with Meal + beef + veggie dinner - ½ of Sue Flannigan alleged First Edition - Gary + Crum - + Boulder lady who steals 1½ million -- See "Without a Trace" - Screaming woman disappears with wild sex man - agent calls him - See some news - Harold Ford is talking crazy - Dog man changed - Cop killed dog - after kids + him -

Where will you leave your wealth?
—Isaiah 10:3 (NAS)

JANUARY 22

WHEN AND HOW CAN I GROW IN MY GENEROSITY TO OTHERS?

Devo - 2 puzzles - lifted weights - Jacked George little solitaire - shot at squirrel saw news - one Raymond - Cite early - went to Britt's game which they won - he played great - scoring, scrapping - feeding - rebounding - Home to annoying Monk -- who was robbed & beaten - Keller murders pregnant girlfriend - Bee attacks - bulletin picture finds Monk - see some House + news —

Stern's colleen calls to remind me of surgery - No word from Steve Caldwell - He deposits Inderwood check to his account.

JANUARY 21

> "In your anger do not sin": Do not let the sun go down while you are still angry, and do not give the devil a foothold. —EPHESIANS 4:26–27 (NIV)

HOW CAN I RELEASE UNRESOLVED ANGER IN MY RELATIONSHIPS?

Buzz. Deco- Walk with Ann & Margie - Do Stretches - Watch Ky beat S. Carolina by 2 - thanks to Rondo's 3 pointer with 1.5 seconds left in game. S. Carolina led by 11 with some 8 minutes left Sparks hits 3 - 3's - one from about 40 ft late in 2nd half -- pump pool cover - Talk to Steve Caldwell - says Lee will be here tomorrow -
Some Solotonic - listen to Bible & talk with Ann about Hebrews Mark & Margie watch game with me - see 3hr. Lincoln- story -
U Conn beats Louisville at L. -
Duke loses to Georgetown - Pillsbury beaten - No unbeatens left.
Rain this AM - & tomorrow

Therefore encourage one another and build one another up. . . . —I Thessalonians 5:11 (RSV)

JANUARY 24

DO I RECOGNIZE THOSE WHO OFFER ENCOURAGEMENT IN MY LIFE?

Up 7:45 - Devo - Started puzzle - got all keys - but can't get 3 impossibles. Go to 7rst Evan w/ Rami - Margi + Mark - Alan - Home to Puzz - ate M Cereal lunch - nap - Rain - Start watching Pittsburg beat Denver. - Some News - Stretch twice & left cough - Kids shopping for dinner - Annabriny cooked chicken from Sam's - eat yogurt - but very hungry - have chicken thigh & leg. - Salad - sherry ice cream - See Without a Trace - last of which I'd seen before - Man confesses & spends 7 yrs. in prison - Student infatuated with her - lets her slip over cliff -
Call Steve Caldwell - doesn't come by - says he will be at Breakfast tomorrow -

January 25

I have learned the secret of being content in any and every situation. . . . —Philippians 4:12 (NIV)

Am I aware of the many blessings in my life?

Slept good - Devo & 2 Puzzles - Am gais Solitaire - Read some of Pace + Masters info - lie around - Arm swells so I take off splint sling - Eat chicken & two cereals - See Sue Thomas - Some still standing - Early Edition - Much of S. Carolina win over Fla - See CSI repeat - had only seen some of it before - See news - Get call from Betty Joplin & Chas. Burris who has had recent cancer skin surgery - Lois not doing too well - Mary Wilson leaves hospital - Call Steve Caldwell — suppose to come by here Friday - doesn't sound good... Can't get tape to work.

They have ears, but they hear not. . . .
—Psalm 115:6

JANUARY 26

HOW CAN I LISTEN TO THE NEEDS OF MY NEIGHBORS?

Devo - Two Puzzles
Ann all A.M. at 1st Pres.
Read pacer material
Call Steve Caldwell - says he's coming tomorrow - Solitaire - Bubba & Ruth over for lengthy talk - We go to Ike's for dinner -
See some Raymond - old car purchase - Frank stole Robert's boots - Marie embellishes card euchre game - "Would you let me in..?" Ray
Eat chicken & Rice with Mark who saw Britt's basketball game - He scores a lot but they lose -
See Sue Thomas - catch drug sellers - 'Elvis' part - See Gary's blond leave & take her kid - Gary finds bombs - in car & at Sun Times -
- Without a trace - 14 yr. old abused by mother - blames Dad - Teacher's Dad - who kills his wife - kills self - Teacher leaves with boy -

January 27

For anyone who enters God's rest also rests from his own work, just as God did from his.
—Hebrews 4:10 (NIV)

Lord, thank You for the blessings of the love between mother and child.

up early - allergy head - tc deod + 2 puzzles - To lunch with Bubba - Al - Carolyn - Ruth Ann - Enjoyed - Al paid - flirted with hostesses + lady in fancy skirt - "you made my day"! - Home to TV - Green Dolphin Street - Lana Turner + Donna Reed - New Zealand Maoris + Van Heflin - Raymond - News - Eggs + bacon - See - some hospital Pree - further reading - some Grizzlies + Closer to home - Monk - one Miracle - guardian angel slaps ear -- Numbers about stolen kidneys - News - man in S. Haven - shooting @ E. High -

That the soul be without knowledge, it is not good.... —Proverbs 19:2

JANUARY 28

WHAT QUESTIONS CAN I TAKE TO GOD IN PRAYER?

Puzzle + 1000 — Ann + Ruth go shopping I'm alone most of day because they go again in Afternoon See Basketball — Game on eve — Louisville beaten by Villanova — UNS + Duke easy winners — Maryland loses See - Cold Case — Mafia Movie with Paul Newman + Tom Hanks — lots of killings — Numbers — seen before - assassin on loose — Drink water + lose it. Milk + Choc lunch — cereal breakfast — Margie feels bad — get nap —

January 29

Pride goes before destruction, and a haughty spirit before a fall. —Proverbs 16:18 (RSV)

LORD, HELP ME TO BE A HUMBLE SERVANT TO OTHERS.

Up for bananas & bread breakfast - Devo. + start puzzle Black suit to church. Guest speaker = great. Home to watch Arkansas jump to 17 pt. lead & Ky. comes back to win by 2 - great team effort - fight hard in 2nd half - Sparks = great - Rondo & big center - whew - Tigers came back often in play-off.

Some solitaire - finish puzzle. Kids + Sue over for dinner - Britt comes late - visited Scott - Sarah. See Movie of real violence - one man whips 2 dozen with fists - See Crusader Jordan - will kids - Muggsie daughter of head cop - he pours out his whiskey. Lots more violence in City -

I can do all things through Christ which strengtheneth me. —PHILIPPIANS 4:13

JANUARY 30

WHAT NEW GOALS CAN I SET FOR MYSELF TODAY?

Worked puzzles after devo – Ruth calls twice about puzzle answers from Fla. on road – Ann went to exercise & Ikes & shopped – worried about her – she should have called. Pumped pool over. Ann goes to small group – I listen to Bible & work puzzles – some solitaire. The Green guy her to do yard – look at new Brokerage papers – Work home puzzle –
Ann to small group –
I shave & go to Britt's eighth grade honor and see him play in "S" Tall game – Home to Raymond + dinner with Mark. See Sue Thomas + 24 hrs – some of Early Edition –
More bad news on TV.

January 31

When he saw the crowds, he had compassion on them, because they were harassed and helpless, like sheep without a shepherd.

—Matthew 9:36 (NIV)

Do I bring compassion to the relationships in my life?

Lost of Meatto Bevo &
2 puzzles - cereal -
Ann off to CWF - I nap
& French puzzle - Ruth calls
Africa on road to check on words - USA
I feel full-headed with allergy +
dripping nose - Stagger - - Talk to
Lazy Mesa - & David - lost Millissa
Send in Morgan Keegan forms -
Ann does check balance - Talk to
brokers who have Ann's stock
- nap again - see Raymond - & eat
soup - See Sue Thomas - + Early Edition
+ Bush's State of Union speech
& Dem response - See News on
school closings -

And whosoever will, let him take the water of life freely. —REVELATION 22:17

FEBRUARY 1

HOW CAN I ACCEPT MY BLESSINGS WITH A GRATEFUL HEART?

Read 2 two Puzzles -
Ann to exercise and Gideon -
2 cereals for Breakfast - lunch
See for Lee and they gal Judy
+ Issue Kelly - then Brigadoon - Kelly
Van Johnson + Cyd Cyrisse
See some Raymond - Puzzle with Ann
- Some solitaire - Hamburger for dinner
Watch Kentucky beat Miss. State -
Great 3 point shooting - Sparks has
25 - See CSI New York - Music
Murder - in pasta boys

Talk to Sharon Wilson + Bobby
McGraw about Pace maker -
I can drive tomorrow -

Sharon gave Curtis Shrenkin'
No money to give last year -
Rent this summer -

FEBRUARY 2

That which is far off, and exceeding deep, who can find it out? —ECCLESIASTES 7:24

DO I REMEMBER A CHILDHOOD EXPERIENCE THAT HELPED TO SHAPE MY LIFE?

Devo & 2 puzzles - Ann to Church - bath & shave - off to Church with Ann - sit with Bubba - see Ewings - Ann's student - went to Stern's for I'm test after lunch - call Steve & Gregg Mason for check clearance. Can mow drive - Rained all night & most of day. - Bobo Harding to Ruth's game in rain - They win easily over 7th grade team - Go in wrong Gym - with brunette fan. Home & Rice & Pork with Marsh & see 1/2 Sue Thomas - all of Early Edition & lady cop - Gary retrieves diamond. Brunette cop bright & pressing see Without a Trace - grapes rape innocent -

Know ye that the Lord he is God: it is he that hath made us, and not we ourselves; we are his people, and the sheep of his pasture. —PSALM 100:3

FEBRUARY 3

WHEN AM I REMINDED OF GOD'S UNCONDITIONAL LOVE FOR ME?

Devo + 2 puzzles - Call Steve's back, Receive Less Mason check by Fed EX + go deposit in Bank - see Delores + give candy - Go by Mercedes + Wes fixes light - I come home + fix Cemi's - - Talk to Wes about sun + coffee Mark's expertise of Engineering - see. Untouchables - get Capone - - Sean wins Oscar - Drive in Rain to Rinse car + verse - See end of Heat of the Night - q sure Raymond - Eat Kelly's lentil soup - See some Rotersperer - (Ghost) - Close to Home - Dominating Mom + Killer son - . He had reason - Neighbor was getting too much of Mom's time - Realter about to sell home - Mom sees him with bloody hammer -
Merle - pretty stupid - diamond hunt -
More deps, inside corruption -

February 4

Bless the Lord, O my soul . . . who heals all your diseases. . . . —Psalm 103:2–3 (RSV)

Where do I see God addressing my physical needs?

Cereal for lunch - Devo & Rom. Puzzle - Penn St. beat Illinois - Louisville & Duke win in OT. Kentucky trounced by Florida - Britt stars in B.B. victory at St. Geo. Episcopal - Mark over for game - Eat salmon & Fruit Salad dinner - Ann won't let me drive - Thanks to Britt - The entire day wasn't ruined -

*I will proclaim the name of the Lord.
Oh, praise the greatness of our God!*
—Deuteronomy 32:3 (NIV)

FEBRUARY 5

AM I TOO FOCUSED ON MY OWN DESIRES?

Devo - v Big Puzzle off to 1st Evan. - Mark & Margie there - checkout hospital call & get gas for Ann - carrying old Visa card - Got Britt over for sack job - See Schee Munk - Super Bowl goes to Steelers over Seattle Seahawks - odds go against Seahawks - see some of Calif. Geo. O'Brien silent film - & another Munk on plane & Raped Prisoner on CSI -

News - Hegenton involved in Atlanta scandal - murders continue - Ann has vast too clothes for family.

FEBRUARY 6

Be ye of an understanding heart. —Proverbs 8:5

AM I OPEN-MINDED IN MY RELATIONSHIPS WITH OTHERS?

Dev. + Puzzles Ann to exercise - Get to Auto check - ate Cerea - - posses - md cereal for lunch - Ann to circle - 2 hour nap - listen to Bible - Mark + Margie over - for left overs. See remedy of cats & pretty wife - - see some of Louisville's loss to Cincy - Texas ive Texas Tech - - see some of producers during Early Edition Show - CSI Miami - Black detective dates white employee. - Murder of six couples killed same way -
Willie looks guilty in Atlanta bombing case - He will testify in Ga.

And your ears shall hear a word behind you, saying, "This is the way, walk in it." . . .
—Isaiah 30:21 (RSV)

FEBRUARY 7

IN WHAT WAYS DOES MY FAITH SUSTAIN ME WHEN I ENCOUNTER HARDSHIPS?

Devo + Puzzles —
Move to Wild Oats
Alco + Drugs for Rejuvenation —
Nap — puzzle — went to 15-tr/15
losing Tourney game — then Home & watch
TN beat Ky by 8 — —
See House + extended news —
Mark + Margie over —
Behind by 10 — Ky got lead — only
to lose it — Poor shooting —

FEBRUARY 8

Blessed are they that mourn: for they shall be comforted. —MATTHEW 5:4

HOW DO I RESPOND TO THOSE WHO ARE EXPERIENCING GRIEF?

Up early to Baptist for peace-maker test - resting place - on to Stern for Lisa's treatment - to Wall Mart for dozen roses to divide up among Stern girls - Ann took Betty J & friends to B.D. lunch. I eat cereal & later naps. Can Meco exercise - Jim. Go to see Joan Pratt as hubby has bleeding attack .. (Mrs) Hughes there - with her Jim's son from Marks, Miss. Civil Eng... Home to Shrimp & ham cheese Sandwich with fruit salad - Chan Meditation - love of Christ - to music I was hearing on disc. Call Caldwell & he says I can deposit check on his loan - call Mark & Marge about David Raines transfer - can't get Kelly - Putei - see Sue Pherney with married boy-friend - Early Edition with Hobson in jail - accused of killing scandal writer... take cot tab & Ann rubs ointment on back - see news - dog can dial 911 - on phone -

For unto us a child is born, unto us a son is given. . . . —ISAIAH 9:6

FEBRUARY 9

IN WHAT WAYS CAN I SHARE THE JOY OF THE NATIVITY THROUGHOUT THE YEAR?

Devo - 2 Puzzles
Go to see Jim Pratt
at Germ. Methodist - Talked
Over there — prayed for him - To 1st
Swan w/ Ann - Patty there with Bubba
Dr. Howard Clark sits with us again -
Back to Pratt - He's asleep when
Ann & I go in to see him - Down to
Cafe. looking for Joan Pratt - upstairs
to find her with Beards - can't get
Joanie to go home with us. - Jim's
son + nurse wife show up - 2nd wife or
more?
Home to Nap - I go to bank w/
Steve's check & deposit it -
Coffee + some solitaire - Mark &
Marie over for fish dinner - see ½
of Sue Thomas + 2nd part of Early
Edition - A bad cop + Lab Doctor
Guilty - Cop lady arrives in time
to save Barry.
see 'Track' + news —

FEBRUARY 10

Withhold not good . . . when it is in the power of thine hand to do it. —Proverbs 3:27

WHAT SMALL GESTURE CAN I PERFORM TODAY THAT WILL BLESS SOMEONE TOMORROW?

Devo - 2 puzzles. Bring in Garbage cans - Snows most of day - 2.3 inches - All kids get home safely - Breeze tonight - some solitaire - See most of Oklahoma - great show. Do stretches. Get bacon & eggs dinner - see Host Whisperer - Kids ghosts still in old house - see Close to home - Numbers - Starlet does the killing. News shows pollutants - Ann to games for Steele -

Ann works up bill paying. More money in bank than I dreamed - Haven't heard from Steve's check yet - call from Diaz about hymn - to whom I took Ann's tulips - meet Henry's daughter.

However, our God turned the curse into a blessing. —Nehemiah 13:2 (NKJV)

February 11

DO I NEED TO CULTIVATE PATIENCE AS I WAIT FOR GOD'S PLANS TO UNFOLD?

Devo – Puzzle – work to music – 2 stretch sessions – one arm weight lift – Talk to Jim Wilson about Erick test drain problem – See Duke overcome Maryland – Ky loses to Vandy by 3 – can't shoot fouls – Fla over LSU @ Fla – some solitaire – back better – Past of House – Clean & frozen – – snow melts – flossed teeth – Read some from Flip – Switch – See Green Mile – & Christie – some Miracle –

FEBRUARY 12

"And as you say, older men like me are wise. They understand." —JOB 12:12 (TLB)

WHAT QUALITIES IN OTHERS DO I ADMIRE AND STRIVE TO EMULATE?

Work Puzzle after Dev - To Church - Market Mackie - Gun out Candy - Home to nap + part of Stuie - Pro-Bowl in Hawaii Kristen's B.D party - cook steak better Maybe out in cold - see over but no Nealey or girlfriend - see some Cace men + dog fights - Huge Cen. adventure in Kuwa & Vietnam over Miss - Eat far too much

He shall gather the lambs with his arm, and carry them in his bosom. . . . —ISAIAH 40:11

FEBRUARY 13

WHEN I AM CONCERNED ABOUT MY LOVED ONES, DO I TRUST THEIR CARE TO THE LORD?

Devo + 2 puzzles
Ann to exercise - + afternoon
Small group - I stretch
Terri + nap - sot here -
Read some of golf book
Mark + Marge over - see ½ hr
comedy + 24 hours --- CSI Miami
Hubby kills lover of 3 women
including wife - to senator who
takes $500 bribe gets off in Nashville
Elves ain't working -

February 14

Love one another deeply, from the heart.
—I Peter 1:22 (NIV)

AM I GENEROUS IN EXPRESSING MY LOVE TO OTHERS?

Devo - 1½ puzzles - Stretch - got call from Ann reminding me of My Jemison's [?] — from 11:20 - tel 3:00 - Then go to Walmart in Germantown pike for Roses for Eva & Ann. Home to some solitaire & news - Sue Raymond & Margie bring gifts to Ann & me - Scrambled eggs for supper - & see Thomas & crazy (dreamy) Early Edition - well in bed to music for near 30 min. See news -

Call Bootie & Bob & Mary Jo were there celebrating with card game -

> "O Lord, forgive! . . . For your sake, O my God, do not delay, because your city and your people bear your Name." —Daniel 9:19 (NIV)

February 15

Do I practice my faith in a way that encourages others?

Puzzles - Devo -
~~Went to Hosp~~ @ Baptist w/ Rose for Nedo Lewis & L Estelle & prayed for Gabley Jim Driver who was confusing nurses. Then to Keiko's - 2 cereal meals & tough steak sandwich for supper. Gee saw Thomas with serial killer - shot by lover-boss when ready to strangle her - See Early edition w/ twin sisters - one a thief - the other with amnesia - Crew charges Gary the full amount but they save him $25.00 - the same of Herman blitz on London & some CSI New York. Ky. over Ga by 8 at UK? - not on TV.

FEBRUARY 16

We are more than conquerors through him who loved us. —ROMANS 8:37 (NIV)

LORD, HELP ME TO EVALUATE SUCCESS ON YOUR TERMS, NOT THE WORLD'S.

Devo - Puzzles - Read ½ Exodus - Stretch - Go to 1st. Svce but leave Banquem lunch before I go - Go to Ins. bldg. to find Girls - but evidently wrong bldg - Home just before Ann arrives from her Ind Pres. meet + lunch - some solitaire - I help Ann with Puzzle - Steve Caldwell calls - says he will bring my loan money tomorrow - See Betty art. + Eat with Meblen + old men - Preacher from E. Methodist Church in Germantown preaches on Truth - got a bow with Mark - See Sug Thomas - Early Edition + put of Jessely blond - Bad weather coming. Johnson nurse calls - need P. in for communion.

So do not throw away your confidence; it will be richly rewarded. —HEBREWS 10:35 (NIV)

FEBRUARY 17

GOD, I BRING MY STRUGGLES TO YOU WITH FULL FAITH.

Devo - 1½ puzzles - Go early to Stern fw Blood test - (2.) see Rachel with cold - Gave out candy - Home to m. & cereal meal - listen to Bible tape - naps - Do to P.O. + Fresh Market + Alco's - for milk cream - Scanner - Omars - give candy - Home to 2 solitaire rubbers + news - Do Doerr's form - Here that Steve's K.C. is at Lethbridge - Bad check returned - See game of Abe Lincoln in Illinois with Raymond Massey - was electric - See a bit of Raymond + Mary Higgins dark mystery - Father kills people who could have saved her + cop - killer - Her grand'ma - + her soft ball throw knocks killer down - cop frees sleeping father -

February 18

> "If your eyes are good, your whole body will be full of light." —Matthew 6:22 (NIV)

Am I seeing clearly the good in my life?

7 commercial puzzles + devo — stretched — some solitaire — Marleo Margie over for Ky. victory over S. Carolina — unexpected — Arkansas beats Florida — work puzzle with Ann — stretch again — walk in house for 28 minutes — see News + Nostradamus + who framed Roger Rabbit — see Edgar Casey — predictions all close to coming — earth changes in way — Casey wanted us to know about changes we need to make with earth and each other — Very cold + icy — 150 wrecks today.

He said to them, "Go into all the world and preach the good news to all creation."
—Mark 16:15 (NIV)

FEBRUARY 19

WHAT KIND OF LEGACY WILL I LEAVE FOR THE WORLD?

Devo - + Big Puzzle - Stretch - lift weight - Solitaire - vaced living Rm Den + Sun-Room - Kitchen - Ann unclogs small sink - Read Book of Hebrews + Bible Dictionary on Melchizedek - + other Abraham Put on fire for kids - Have turkey + veggies - sw potato concoction! See Olympic skaters - some pro basketball call sites games - dumps - walk 30 minutes - Saw of Murder by Numbers with - brunette detective I like - Looked awfully thin - Sandra Bullock -

FEBRUARY 20

There is no authority except that which God has established.... —ROMANS 13:1 (NIV)

DO I SOMETIMES FORGET THAT GOD IS MY ONE TRUE LEADER?

2 Nuzzlers + Deer - Stretch twice today + walk in house - Thawing outside - Ann works hard on balancing for our Tax report - Read some from Flip Switch diet book and from Prevention. See news after working puzzle with Ann - See some Raymond.

Mark + Mary come over - We see Sue Thomas (continued) & 24 hrs. - also CSI Miami - Woman killed with nail gun - son does it - overhearing her bid to have Dad killed - News - Big fire at roller rink - Find for on TV with black senator from North -

Talk to Colleen about increase in drugs.

*To every thing there is a season,
and a time to every purpose under the heaven.*
—Ecclesiastes 3:1

February 21

HOW CAN I CHERISH THE UNIQUE CHALLENGES AND OPPORTUNITIES OF THIS STAGE IN MY LIFE?

Devos + 2 puzzles — Go with Ann to P.O. for Marge. To Akes for drugs + Ann to $1 store — To Fresh Market for salmon & fruit — Ann to Stewart & Michaels. Stretch boxes — call drug store for 05 drug records — Herricane for fax + Screen service — Wrote !! Motter puzzle & see news — Raymond — see Horaces 2nd part — Early edition diamond steal — J CSI in LA — daughter a prostitute — & future mayor tells prostitute — daughter left behind — News — Miss State Arab student arrested for terror plans — Mps Air Part — Talk to Mark — Marg called —

FEBRUARY 22

> Now it is required that those
> who have been given a trust must prove faithful.
> —I Corinthians 4:2 (NIV)

DO I INSPIRE OTHERS WITH THE TRUST THAT I PLACE IN THEM?

Stretched - Deoo & off to exercise - Charlotte has daughter-in-law & two kids - Charlotte & Leeo to Shoots & Book Store - for hamburger & yogurt & Jello - After lunch - Talk to Andrew about Ann's sloth - & all these Caldwells who say he will pay - off his debt tomorrow -

Go with Ken & Betty to Hamburger dinner - Back to see Thomas + TV victory over Fla @ Fla - See Early Edition - Mary helps the blinded - rescues little boy - is in turn rescued by or elsewhile villain - See Monty-Python stuff - & News of Republican rep. confessing & getting a one yr. sentence -

For ye know the grace of our Lord Jesus Christ, that, though he was rich, yet for your sakes he became poor. . . . —II Corinthians 8:9

FEBRUARY 23

DO I PRACTICE GIVING TO OTHERS AS DILIGENTLY AS I MIGHT?

Devo - can't do Today - who could? - Ann to Church - Stretch - Go to 1st Evan - Lunch - to Brokers - see Sandra Tuttnell - No Steve - No answer to call -- Nap while Bible Listening - Sa Bride -- News - Eat Spaghetti with Micah - No Macy - see repeat on Sue Thomas - 'Enlightenment' - - Early Edition - News visitor from New York - Lected of delivery - Gary under surveillance - see 48 hrs. - sound off for while -

FEBRUARY 24

Train a child in the way he should go, and when he is old he will not turn from it.
—Proverbs 22:6 (NIV)

DO I SHOW LOVE AND PATIENCE TO THOSE AROUND ME?

Puzzles — News — While Ann shops for clothes & Groceries — See S. Pacific on T.V. Mitzi, John Kerr & Brazzi — Play Bridge — Steve Caldwell calls & puts me on phone with Bank exec. Big relief — I'm glad I didn't call his wife as I had planned — Bad cough & sore neck treated by heat pad & neck pillow.
See. Movie — Karate Kid — who wins over bullies & cheating coach. See Numbers & part of old movie & Kelly does in Ambassador over 1 dead wifes jewelery in los ruin coats

I will guide thee with mine eye. —Psalm 32:8

FEBRUARY 25

ARE THERE SPECIAL PLACES IN MY HOME THAT REMIND ME OF CHERISHED PEOPLE AND EVENTS?

Devo + 1 puzzle - Stretch - walk - See Louisville lose and Ky to LSU - close turnovers - and shot beat us Mark + Maggie over to supper then it played bridge - Beth Lyons sick -- see 2 summer wives & Numbers - but miss who letter was why? See bear friend later killed by me + girl -

FEBRUARY 26

I, even I, am he that comforteth you....
—Isaiah 51:12

When did I last reach out to someone who was suffering?

Devo - Puzzle -
To 1st Evan -
Have to stretch or
walk - see games
eed Fla - UConn over Villanova -
Kennedy mystery - 2 cars
- Family over for dinner -
See Spider Man - - Some need
Ann turns pool pump off for me
- Ferring + Kelly see Margie off -
for me - Old news - letter treacalti
coming -

> "He is able to humble those who walk in pride."
> —Daniel 4:37 (NAS)

FEBRUARY 27

How might I put my pride to the side, even if just for today?

Devo + Big Murph — To Exercise + see Eric M. with broken arm — To P.O. with Ann where she hits curb + cries — Home — stretch + walk after long nap — Ann to dentist and to circle meet — see News + Raymond — Mark + Margie over — See Sue Thomas and 24 hrs. — CTU prevents death of Mrs. Cumberbatch & president's wife — Workers overseen boss to get agents on scene — STU finds source of gas & his life attempted with bomb — Becky's slandered friend puts on good show —

Teachers being attacked in schools — Mardi Gras put on in N.O. — school burned in Ark — Collierville trouble with developer —

February 28

Whatever your hand finds to do, do it with all your might.... —Ecclesiastes 9:10 (NIV)

Is there a simple pleasure that will brighten my outlook today?

Puzzles - forgot dogs - Ann off to CWF - I study letters and go to Morgan Keegan - Sterns. After lunch to Bank with Ann's check. To Ikes for drug - To Dollar Store for cotton balls. Got Tay Urine at Germantown Hardware - To Wild Oats for cereal & tomato - - Home to Migraine Nap - do Stretch. Read deering commercials - see former cop killing drug dealers on Sue - Gary and Irish visitors - Get agent out of garbage who marries wandering girl - 2 Rubbers - and news.

Then will I sprinkle clean water upon you, and ye shall be clean.... —Ezekiel 36:25

MARCH 1

AM I EXPERIENCING THE JOY OF GOD'S PURIFYING LOVE?

Puzzles - To exercise - Ques Alups - & listen to Luke c17 & Map - walk 30 min. & stretch - but eggs & bacon supper with fruit - Watched Ky beat TN by 2 pts - Morris & Rondo stars - good defense - great victory - Mark over for last ½ - see some of Early Edition & some CSI N.y & stupid English Monte Python. Robberies & shootings continue in Memphis. Read great stories from Huidpost —

MARCH 2

Thou art my father, my God, and the rock of my salvation. —Psalm 89:26

DEAR LORD, REMIND ME OF YOUR REASSURING NEARNESS.

Ann to me Pres -
Devo - 2 Puzzles
Stretch - listen to Bible
& walk - Go to 1st Evan.
with Ann for lunch sermon - sat by
Preacher -- Home to Music & Nap +
Puzzle with Ann - Got leaves off
pool -- See Raymond. Mark & Margie
over for soup. See Sue Thomas -
Hobson and 48 hrs.
Memphis beaten by U A B by 6 pts.
Texas, Duke & TN. lose last night -
See end of Mps. game - they
were out-hustled. Mps players foul
shots put it away - lost his man
& has her picture tattooed on his arm.

Let him have all your worries and cares, for he is always thinking about you and watching everything that concerns you. —I Peter 5:7 (TLB)

March 3

DO I KEEP MY EYES ON THE ROAD AHEAD AS I NAVIGATE LIFE?

Walked in house - then a stretch - do to Mayor's class party - Magic tricks cool - but they are too high to pay much attention to stories - tried to get Ann's gas - too crowded at White Station & Poplar - Eat shrimp for supper -

MARCH 4

The Lord will watch over your coming and going both now and forevermore. —PSALM 121:8 (NIV)

WHICH JOYS IN MY LIFE WERE BLESSINGS SENT IN DISGUISE?

Walked with Marge & Ann - see Abbey & pet her -- naps - watch games - UConn over Louisville - TN beats Vandy Memphis over Houston - Miss St. beat Alabama - Ol' Miss loses by 3 to LSU. - See the Beautiful Mind Crowe plays schizo genius who wins Nobel prize - nearly drowns baby - sees imaginary people - finally ignores them - has wife who loves him -

> "And if you greet only your brothers, what are you doing more than others?"
> —Matthew 5:47 (NIV)

MARCH 5

How might I make a newcomer feel welcome?

Started Puzz. after Devo + Funnies + glance @ programs — To 1st Even — and home to see Ky's lethargic play in losing to Fla. @ Home — no scoring — rebounding — pitiful — upsets all around —

Blow pool cover before rain which does come @ night. Stretch + walk — Sue brings over pork rump Bar-b-Q very good... see some of Caddy Shack — finish puzzle — some Bridge — Mikey + Lydia absent in Huntsville — see Sherlock Holmes — Tape last part for Mark — TN. Waltz people seen on tape taking money —

MARCH 6

And because ye are sons, God hath sent forth the Spirit of his Son into your hearts, crying, Abba, Father. —GALATIANS 4:6

HOW OFTEN DO I REST IN GOD'S PRESENCE?

Devo - 2 puzzles - Elderly 1½ - walk - Listen to MARK's chap. + doze off - Call David Raines - and Stern Clinic - Looks like I can do it all now - Some weight lift - Bridge - solitaire. Ann to circle - Margie cooks dinner - Mark & I watch 24 hrs. + I see Miami Vice. More murders in Memphis? - Move on video signing - Ann gets Marie-french check. - No news from Steve - although he says I'll get loan back - M. drugs in town - Bath & razor shave -

She looketh well to the ways of her household, and eateth not the bread of idleness.
—Proverbs 31:27

MARCH 7

Do I set a positive example for those who are younger?

Devo — 2 Puzzles — Go walk with Ann — Do stretch — 2 cereal meals — Mark calls + I advise him to have this intestine exam — Go to Ike's for drugs — give out candy. Verify young man optometrist was on T.V. ad — Sit here — get drugs — Buy 2 plants — one for Tamara + one for Ann — See Jeremy + Vel — To with OEB Fresh Garden for fruit — Salmon — forget milk — Home to Outer Bridge Run over creek — @ Phys. Therapy — See news + Raymond when Marie tells them she will move. See Sue Thomas + dancing master caught. See House in heart transplant some Gary Hobson — art thinks Dr. —

MARCH 8

> Clothe yourselves with compassion, kindness, humility, gentleness and patience.
> —Colossians 3:12 (NIV)

AM I DEDICATED TO SEEING THE GOOD IN THE PEOPLE AROUND ME?

Devo - Today Puzzle - Stretch - To Exercise - Home - To Clay John's Home - then to store for Milk & Juice - gas up Cenny's car - Home - wash two cars - See some news - Raymond - Family kicked out of retirement home - then - Raymond gets angry say - Mark & Mary over for Cenny's beef & beans recipe - See See Furies + Early Edition - CSI NY. + then dump. - To bed -

But godliness with contentment is great gain.
—I Timothy 6:6 (NIV)

MARCH 9

FOR WHAT BLESSINGS IN MY LIFE AM I UNCONDITIONALLY THANKFUL?

Devo — Today Puzzle — Stretch — Run to 2nd Pres — Bath — We go to 1st Cobon — See Gordon Round — Bubba + Patty — Also 3 from Minnesota — Home to see Kg — Fight by Ol' Miss — Face Alabama tomorrow —
Eat BLT — walk a bit — Talk to Mark — Margie with headache —
See repeat Sue Thomas & Russian Mafia — See Early Edition with Maggie — + dog — See Missing Mystery — 2 lesbians as it turns out — girl locked in bowling alley — U Conn upset by Syracuse — Vandy wins over Auburn (tough) Ga. beaten by Arkansas —
No news from Steve —

MARCH 10

"Remember the Lord in a distant land, and think on Jerusalem." —JEREMIAH 51:50 (NIV)

WHAT SYMBOLS OF MY FAITH ARE MOST IMPORTANT TO ME?

Devo - 1 puzzle - Run with Mark to his his colonoscopy - I stretch & walk - no weights - See Syracuse upset U Conn - also Ky. over Bama after 21-22 1st half - 5 parts & buddies let 3's - win by 8, after being down 10 with 5 min. & so -. Vandy loses to LSU - Fla winning over Ark - see some close to home - woman murderer found guilty - took up with parson & stabs guard -- she faced seizure situation - helped in robberies - see Mark with dentist killer & assist... - Lieut. saves him by going to office - Bonds stolen.

> "I have set before you an open door, and no one can shut it. . . ." —Revelation 3:8 (NKJV)

MARCH 11

WHAT OBSTACLES HAVE I BEEN ALLOWING TO HOLD ME BACK?

Devo - Cne. puzzle - Ann to Sam's - I go to Ike's - Home depot & Radio Shack for Squirrel aid - Set rat poison and traps of glue - Home to see Ky get beat by S. Carolina - Fla. beats lazy LSU - Syracuse wins Big East Tourney as lowest seed - McNamara (white boy) leads the way. - See Mary Higgins Clarke murder mystery - Dr. learns to transplant faces - morning wife near victim who decides on a new life with Dr. who saved her - More teen murders in Mphs - Frist chose at Peabody convention as best choice for Pres. by meeting Rep. peers -

MARCH 12

And [Jesus] saith unto them, Is it lawful to do good on the sabbath days . . . ? —MARK 3:4

HOW DOES MY FAITH INSPIRE ME TO DO GOOD WORKS THROUGHOUT THE WEEK?

Puzzle - Devo - Bath - off to 1st Ever. with Mary + Mark. Home to cereal after Getting Lydia's B.D. cake at Fresh Market. Then Ann buys Jewelery next door - See 71a. beat S. Carolina by 2. ✓ Iowa beat Ohio State - Bridge + Truss setting - set wren free - Start fire + Mark helps me cook Steak for Lydia's B.D. party - Ken + Betty came by - She + Ann go to Sara's B.D. party - Everyone here for supper... See some of Everest, the death Mountain - Stretch + walk some. Vack some in Kitchen + Den -

> "Do not fear, for I have redeemed you; I have called you by name; you are Mine!"
> —Isaiah 43:1 (NAS)

MARCH 13

DO I REMEMBER GOD'S PRESENCE DURING THE STORMS IN MY LIFE?

Devo - Read James - 2 Puzzles - Pace maker checked by Sterm - O.K. - Air condition unit making noise - Called Herman left message - No word from Cliff. Ann to small group of 3 - Stretched - lifted weights - squirrel must have bought it - Played Bridge - News - one Raymond - Ate steak again Merle & I see Sue & 24 later. 2 dis caulking in Computer to save rest - 16/ln - Kelley - see some Miracle workers & CSI Miami - Girlfriend of Fish eye - is murderess in CSI - Car break-ins & Gang killings

MARCH 14

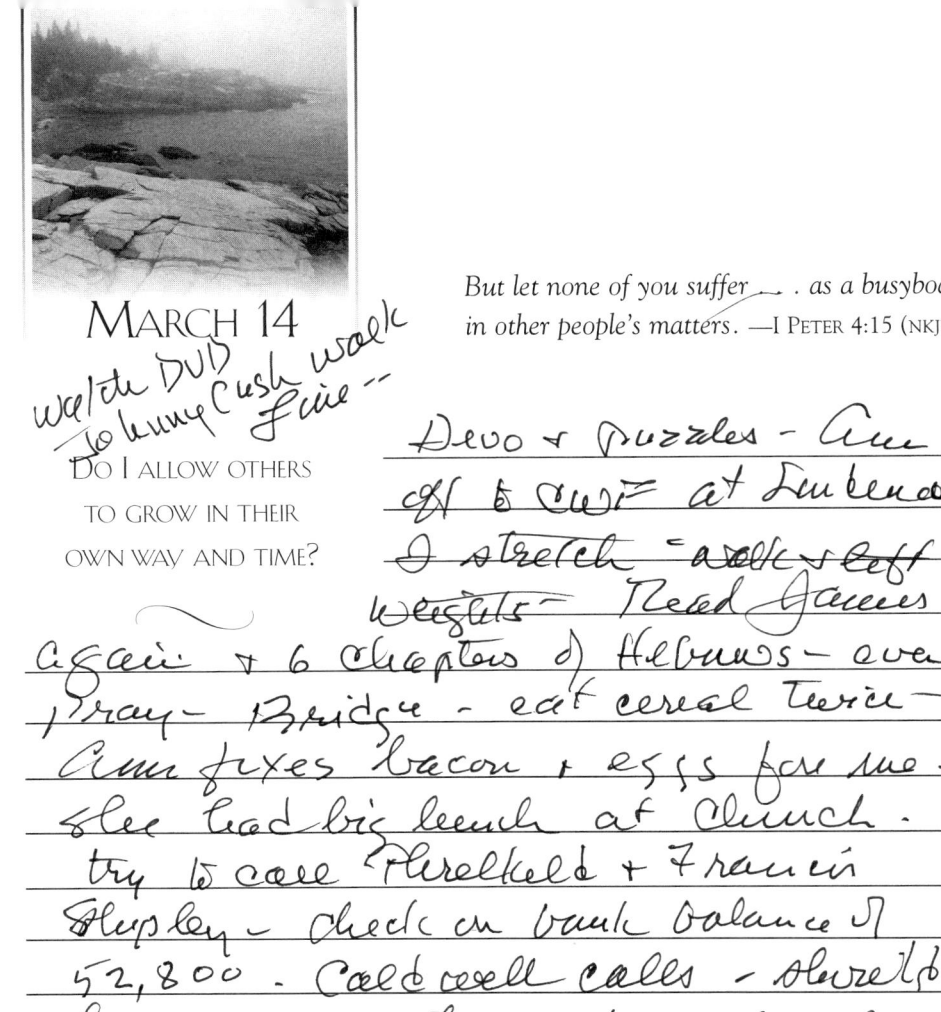

walk DVD
walk Cush walk
to bring Cush Line --

But let none of you suffer ... as a busybody in other people's matters. —I PETER 4:15 (NKJV)

DO I ALLOW OTHERS TO GROW IN THEIR OWN WAY AND TIME?

Devo + puzzles - Ann
off to CWF at Lindenwood
- stretch - walk - lift
weights - Read James
again + 6 chapters of Hebrews - ever
pray - Bridge - eat cereal twice -
Ann fixes bacon + eggs for me -
Glee had big lunch at Church.
try to call Threlkeld + Francis
Shipley - check on bank balance of
52,800 - Caldwell calls - shouldn't
have money this week - almost naps
- stay moving around -
See Sue Thomas catch woman
assassin -- whom only Glee
suspected - Sec. keeps job when
everyone appreciates her - Sister Mile's
resting place -
Gary saves young woman with
fatherless child - Dad comes around
- UFO's frequent Mexico -
Five deaths in Memphis - Teen dies
trying to save two young siblings

We do not know how to pray as we should . . .
—Romans 8:26 (NAS)

MARCH 15

WHAT STEPS CAN I TAKE TO ENRICH MY PRAYER LIFE?

Lift weights - Devo - + 2 puzzles - Stretch - up 7:15 - off to exercise + Home to mid cereal bowl Ann off to shop - & get prescription I go to bank - to Barth Jack for info on ventilator machine - in Rep - Bridge - Read Hebrews and sp to dinner with Joplins and Mus to Mouse - - - Home to Sue Thomas - Early Edit - & Moodices on new Channel & plane over to sleep. Kristi came by to get me on internet - Walked with TU in -

MARCH 16

Open thou mine eyes, that I may behold wondrous things.... —Psalm 119:18

CAN I REMEMBER A TIME WHEN GOD BROUGHT AN UNEXPECTED GIFT INTO MY LIFE?

Up late - Revo & Puzzles - Buth - Go with Ann for Barber & Patty - Hear Howard Clark talk about adultry & sexual diseases - Morality in U.S. going to pot -- Go to Ike's (twice) with cartoons & candy - Some Bridge -- See Raymonds Mom drive car into fence - Then to Italy - We see Sue Thomas with deaf informer - Gary & news reporter - Buddy wins paper & makes big money - Inspected Sea Music and Model head quilting - Seeded teams struggle to win - Geo. Washington - Xavier give Gonzaga fits - Morrison brings 'em through - News 3 black nephews arrested for bank robbery & kidnapping hostage -

> "But when you give to the needy, do not let your left hand know what your right hand is doing, so that your giving may be in secret. Then your Father, who sees what is done in secret, will reward you." —Matthew 6:3–4 (NIV)

MARCH 17

WHAT SECRET ACTS OF KINDNESS CAN I PERFORM?

Devo - 2 puzzles - Britt over to work but watches TV more than works - I stretch - lift weights - walk with Marge & Ann early - Bradley upsets Kansas - Kentucky over UAB - Tough all the way - Tenn. wins last second on Bradshaw goal - NC tough win over Murray State - Michigan State wins upset. UConn has to work hard to win. Mask & Marc over for dinner + game - Ky. shoots poorly but wins with foul shooting - Perry stars on boards and with 25 pts - Sparks 2 crucial foul shots - but terrible from field - Must play # 1 seed U. Conn Sunday -

March 18

Jesus said to him, "Judas, would you betray the son of man with a kiss?" —Luke 22:48 (RSV)

How do I remain loyal to God and those I love?

Devo — Puzzle — walk with Ann & Mary & see Abbey & Mike Bernstein — Fla wins — Tenn. + UCLA — Alabama Lose — Miss oga wins — Big games Tomorrow — Blow leaves off back patio & take leaves off Pool cover — stretch — snake oil — cereal breakfast — Mushroom — salmon & fruit salad supper — ice cream dessert — Ann to store for cream cheese & salmon — Read Guide Post thru — except for Barbara Walters —

Thou, O Lord, art a God full of compassion, and gracious. . . . —PSALM 86:15

MARCH 19

WITH WHOM CAN I SHARE A MESSAGE OF PEACE AND FORGIVENESS?

Duo - Do Puzzle Tight - Stretch & Lift weights - Go to 15th Even - raining - Home to Ball games. Mps. easy winner - Key fights heard before losing to Connecticut - Flem miss last 2 minute foul shots but get the rebound Morris fouls out - Sparks phenomenal with 3's - 28 pts - Good fighting finish - Mark over to watch - checks Key score with field glasses Eat Corned Beef & Cabbage - Marie calls am at supper sit-down time - Shubler calls about Ruth - All over for Corned Beef & Cabbage - See Sundler's - Mr. Deeds comes to town - Woman reporter falls in Love with Deeds - Hear Chan. 10 Special Moment - 4 Jordon - More murders on News -

MARCH 20

The aim of our charge is love that issues from a pure heart and a good conscience and sincere faith. —I Timothy 1:5 (RSV)

DO I STRIVE TO BE GENUINE IN ALL OF MY INTERACTIONS?

1st Day of Spring - Rainy & Cold - Went to Exercise - 2 puzzles stretch & batch before go - Ann to Amicale group - thru Forever - Mail & Margie over for supper - Kristi works on computer - over Rubles - on Outer Bridge - Read Bible Dictionary on Boaz - & various enemies & angels allows Xtians back - Caanan - Boaz - Eat Corn Beef & cabbage - & see Sue Thomas & 24 hrs. - catch girl conspiracies & find alien gassers - See CSI Miami - girls invaded & one shot - News - bit - Run dictation - Bad weather all Day -

"If you are wise, your wisdom will reward you. . . ." —Proverbs 9:12 (NIV)

March 21

AM I UNDERSTANDING AND APPRECIATIVE OF THE DIFFERENCES OF OTHERS?

Devo - Puzzles — Listen to complete Maul. disc - Stretch — walk in house & lift weights - start writing in afternoon — on Sunday School lessons — Leftovers & fruit salad supper — — See old Raymond — Part of see Thomas (repeat) Mom & Dad in town — See Early Edition middle woman — over bridge - body never found - fake shooting — & some of sexy videos — & stupid Wm Powell - Myrna Loy movie with Jack Carson — — Rape talk at White Sulphur & Manassas school — Crack house to be leveled — . — Caldwell calls - Money supposedly on way — old story —

MARCH 22

But grace was given to each of us according to the measure of Christ's gift. —EPHESIANS 4:7 (RSV)

IS THERE A QUIET SOMEONE IN MY LIFE WHO MIGHT HAVE SOMETHING IMPORTANT TO SAY?

Devo - Puzzles - lab breakfast - To Exercise - Meet Presh's daughter - To Davis Kid & bank - Home to drain pool even - Nap - some bridge - stretch - Meant to work leaves but didn't - See Raymond & Super Bowl - see Movie Twins - good - Heist - & some shows this comedy - News - Drug Bust - & many worse - break-ins -

Write some - but Comm & TV break in.

Call Hughes - Burrus - Weary, Lov & Burnettes - Steve still doesn't have money - To be sent to Keeoyer we hope!

Beloved, let us love one another: for love is of God. . . . —I John 4:7

MARCH 23

WHAT IS THE MOST COMPELLING EXAMPLE OF LOVE THAT I HAVE WITNESSED?

Feed- Puzz. Wade + Stretch - No luck lifting on Peter - Budge - call Jack for real help - Jimmy Nelson - Forrest calls - Marge cooks supper - Mark over - We see Mps beat Bradley - Duke beaten by LSU - News about murders - Preacher shot - wife? - Walter Gonzaga lead UCLA - UConn plays Memphis -

MARCH 24

> "Look, I am alive forever and ever!
> And I hold the keys of death and the grave."
> —Revelation 1:18 (NLT)

How am I reminded of Jesus' everlasting love?

Puzzles + Devo - Stretch + Lift weights - cereal + corn beef sandwich for supper - take Ann's check to bank - Give candy ask for keys - 'got me in trouble' - Do some leaves outside - Pull a few weeds - see news - walk Puss. with Ann - Read some Hebrews - Chey calls with Refund - must pay $500 to State - Villanova beats Boston College in OT. by 1 - Fla. + Geo.Town - 2 pts at half - Geo. Mason big winnings over Notre Dame squeeze #14 - Watch games + part of Child Star Bio. - + couple of miracles on 12

Let us throw off everything that hinders and the sin that so easily entangles, and let us run with perseverance the race marked out for us.
—Hebrews 12:1 (NIV)

March 25

What can I do to sharpen my focus on my ultimate goals?

Walk with Margie - Devo - Puzzle - + stretch before she shows up - Jack Jackson here + finds squirrel hole in roof - Takes lawn mower to fix - Give him $200 to buy rock to fix flower beds - See LSU win over Texas in O.T. Memphis plays terrible game losing to UCLA - couldn't shoot - too many fouls + turnovers - Big stars held down by poor shooting + bench time - inexperience shows.

Britt works long in yard - Marg brings him + gets him - see 48 hrs. showing murders reported as suicides in Aruba + Bahamas - Read Annie's (Helen) study - listen to Bible + Marie work - shows up to claim her long lost glasses - Bacon + Egg supper — see some of my best friend's wedding with Julia Roberts - also 7 miracles

MARCH 26

Trust in him at all times; ye people, pour out your heart before him. . . . —PSALM 62:8

GOD, I SUBMIT TO YOUR CARE THE STRUGGLES IN MY LIFE.

Devo - Start USA & walk on way to exercise. Stop @ Kroger for milk etc - Stretch before exercise.

Talk to Steve - says Mickey is near - Also to Clay Isom for Tax business - - May clear $1,000 -

Ann to small group - -

Study Hebrews - with some in house - See woods & one Raymond's Meade & Moore over - Sue Thomas old 24 ers. - CSI Meter games - girl the murderer - & high point girl - Owner to jail for weapons tracks & using group to upgrade games - Rob banks -

Minister's wife in Selmer pleads guilty to husbrip murder -

Be ye thankful. —COLOSSIANS 3:15

MARCH 28

WHO WOULD BE ENCOURAGED BY AN EXPRESSION OF GRATITUDE FROM ME?

Puzzler — Ann off to CWF — Jack Jackson over to fix roof and brought mower back — give him $500 more to do Ann's floral ruins — with Rock — McCabe comes over but offers no help — O little wraglet & stretch — Go out & dig up many bad grass clumps call Steve — no money yet.. Nap — Heat meals — see Raymond — Eat Salmon Beer brings Lusso — See See Thomas — & wife Keith's Husband who's armored car is robbed —

See House — victim's wife trying to poison him.. See Law & Order —
Cops gun son. — & step son he doesn't know about guilty of murder —

March 28

27

"I have come into the world as a light, so that no one who believes in me should stay in darkness."
—John 12:46 (NIV)

ARE MY DECISIONS LED BY MY FAITH?

Ru

The Sovereign LORD is my strength; he makes my feet like the feet of a deer, he enables me to go on the heights.... —HABAKKUK 3:19 (NIV)

MARCH 29

DO I TAKE TIME TO CAREFULLY EVALUATE IMPORTANT TRANSITIONS IN MY LIFE?

Puzzle – exercise – Shop with Ann — Sho take gifts to Board ladies & to Sheri – Get P.N. test & talk to Johnson – Pace Maker site – normal to ecowe leigh heart beat – To Walgreen's for new eye drops — 11. Home to some Bridge – finish puzzle – outside for golf awning. Meet Hallee's new boyfriend – — Ann takes Britt to the dentist. Ev. dine event. – talk to Kelly & Nancy – Get chicken salad & see Sue Thurman – Early Edition and Heist – more Murder news – Look over Ann's lesson for tomorrow –

MARCH 30

> *Your love has given me great joy and encouragement....* —PHILEMON 7 (NIV)

HOW DO I LIFT UP OTHERS WHEN THEY ARE HURTING?

Puzzles - Devo - Stretch with weights & walk. Hot tub on & off to 1st Evan - Ann & I sit with Patti & Bubber. Preach on telling lies of many kinds - Have to Budget & nap. Out in yard - Dig up bad grass and scatter grub worm poison to fight moles. Help Ann tidy up back yard. - Caldwell calls early - no checkup - See Raymond - Mark over for dinner - See Sue Thomas, Early Edition & Without a Trace - Mom abandons kids - 5 yr old tries to keep 'em together - News - Drug busts - Am. woman hostage released -

And he said unto them, Take heed, and beware of covetousness: for a man's life consisteth not in the abundance of the things which he possesseth.
—LUKE 12:15

MARCH 31

DO I NEED TO FREE MYSELF FROM THE HOLD OF MATERIAL THINGS?

Puzzles — Devo. — Went to see Jimmy Fraser — Aunt + brother Bill — in bed 4 wks w/ move —

To Home Depot for Top soil — + clippers weren't there — Home to nap + got edger going on Monkey Grass — Two Trips out — Garbage comes late — Gave 'em candy — Supervisor on the lifting job — Go to Dixie for veggie dinner — See — Nazi hook up with Arabs — Jews embarrass all Middle-East with war victory — Saddam comes out as leader + murders thousands — See close to home — Brother kills brother for wife — she's in on it — They supposedly confess on each other — Crooked developer gets long sentence —

See Tirpitz — Battleships go down — See Numbers — Arab kills lady diplomat — girl agent shoots him down —

April 1

This one thing I do . . . —Philippians 3:13

What is the most important goal that I can accomplish today?

News - Hard commercial
Puzzle - Use edger on
Monkey grass - + blower
- on leaves + dust - Ann +
I bag (2) them out front - She works
on plant patch - Nap - Tuna salad
supper - see Fla. romps over James Mad.
+ UCLA over LSU - no contest -
Daylight saving starts tomorrow -

Read entire Guidepost during games -
some Bridge + Solitaire -
Ann to store -

And after the earthquake a fire; but the Lord was not in the fire: and after the fire a still small voice. —I Kings 19:12

April 2

Do I carve out quiet moments each day so that I can listen for God's voice?

April 3

Pray without ceasing. —I Thessalonians 5:17

What questions can I bring to my conversations with God?

Lift weights - Devo - Start puzzle - off to Exercise - Shop with Cem @ Lowe's & Dollar Tree - cereal lunch - got call from Steve - no lead yet - call McCabe - no preteen - cut front lawn - see news of Tornado devastation & Raymond - Eat with Mark & Margie -- See Sue Tomus. Aussie's Dad reforms - must a heart attack - 48 hrs! - President is the villian - Baby girl saved - See Florida Run all over UCLA. Noah the star " Big men dunk all night " sets final & tourney block record

Thus says the Lord: "Heaven is my throne and the earth is my footstool...." —Isaiah 66:1 (RSV)

APRIL 4

HOW CAN I BRING A MEASURE OF HOPE AND HEALING TO MY SURROUNDINGS?

Devo - Puzzler - wreck my edger - take it to Sears - no help - go to Lees/Moosen for check after talking to David - call for Macabe - Crawley calls about Ashcraft - J talk to Joyce Cole - evidently little or no damage - go to Ski's tires - get haircut - go to bank + sing to Delores - Mail Max's letter -- see some Raymond + Sue Thomas - fires agent who lied about her - See House - girl with tick bite - House's cane sawed in two by Dr. guest - See Miracles - concentration camp brothers - Heart surgery on Chinese baby - no stretch - nap or walk -

APRIL 5

Our Father who art in heaven. . . .
—Matthew 6:9 (RSV)

What feelings does the Lord's Prayer awaken in me?

One Puzzle - News — up late & off to exercise. Home to cereal & call Ann's friends about Jimmy's funeral & visitation. Help Ann with puzzle - off to Sears with busted mower. Traffic blocked on Shady Grove - Doron East to line of cars - turn back & down White & 76Turn - Go to Fresh Market for Salmon, potatoes & bananas - Trip check cry't girl and S Then Home to wash two pother - covered cars - See Hees & CSI plus breed & order — Talk to pres Ashcroft & leave messages for Olds & 1Keys.

The teaching of the wise is a fountain of life....
—Proverbs 13:14 (RSV)

APRIL 6

LORD, THANK YOU FOR THE POSITIVE INFLUENCES IN MY LIFE.

3 Puzzles today - stretch & do receipts - Bath & to Church @ 1st Evan -- Buzz with Ann. who went to 1st Med Presb. All re-dress and go to Jimmy Fraser visitation. Meet Ann's sister & son + others - Virginia Pool. Bev. Kaye Ruth Turner from W.B. Very sad for Ann. Home to some Raymond & Clinton & finish sealed dinner with Mark & Margie - See most of Sue Thomas - Andy Griffith & Much Video - in New York - Ambassador killed ... See child capturing on without a trace - News. thief wrecks stolen car in chase - 7 yr old girl raped by 13 yr old - severe weather coming for tonight & Fri. night.

April 7

"I [wisdom] was his constant delight, laughing and playing in his presence." —Proverbs 8:30 (TLB)

ARE MY EYES OPEN TO THE SOURCES OF PLAYFUL DELIGHT IN MY LIFE?

Devo - impossible 'Today' buzz...
Bad weather threat for 12 hours - 12 people killed by Tornado in Gallatin, near Ruth & Cel - Go to Jimmie Fraser's funeral - sit by Gayle Freeman —
- See News - get Bacon & Egg Supper - see Mystery - aunt. Freeze poisoning - see Closets Home too - Also Miracles & numbers.
111 Jack Jackson works sink & wall paper - fixes my edger -
- looks over landscaping -

> Jesus . . . for the joy that was set before him endured the cross, despising the shame. . . .
> —Hebrews 12:2

APRIL 8

Lord, help me to see the blessings that might come from my struggles.

Can. Puzzle - Pulled Pieces out of front lawn - Bagged leaves & dumped off road. Read - "What am I here for" - Christ is what counts - not me! Ruth Turner calls for Ann Fraser address - Ann out there - groceries + Baskets - Some Bridge & solitaire - Stretch - lift weights - see "Go On Anyway (Alone) Cheryl Ladd — Frances killed in Korea - Marries neighbor - loses son & D. in Law in wreck - Hubby gets Alzheimer - Maud D. starts to leave - comes back for Big Thank-you party - First Love shows up — See some Jackie Gleason -

April 9

And the multitudes that went before, and that followed, cried, saying, Hosanna to the Son of David. . . . —Matthew 21:9

Do I respond with humility as a witness for my faith?

Devo - Puzzles -
To 1st Even. for music celebration - Home & cereal & Backyard work - on pool cover & blow leaves + seed & fill one bag - Do 2nd chap. of Purpose driven life -- Vacuum house - Empty most of dishwasher - Play Bridge + Solitare - Kids over for scupper - Sam's chicken - easier for Ann -. see back end of movie + crossing Jordan - couple of repeat Murders + John Wayne Maureen O'Hara -. Shir Willis - Ed. Buchannan - young Van Dyke - - News - another murder - abusive buddy kicks wife after she files report - Give Kelly + Nancy 4000 IRA money -

My soul is exceeding sorrowful, even unto death.... —Matthew 26:38

APRIL 10

IS MY GRATITUDE TO GOD CONSTANT, EVEN WHEN I AM IN PAIN?

Devo - Purpose Driven Edge front yard - Blow grass & seeds - Bag - Here from Steve Caldwell - scrip check has arrived & will call tomorrow after verification - Very Tired - Take Hot Tub - Win a rubber - Marge over - Mark @ meeting - shows up for last ½ of 2+ hours - see Sue Thomas & CSI Miami - Two thrill killers & Bank murder - cartell leader killed -

Mexicans demonstrate - Law officers out of order - over small dent in car - Mark takes checks - for tomorrow delivery to David Raines -

Tape 2+ hours & give it to him - though he saw last ½ -

APRIL 11

And Jesus . . . touched his ear, and healed him.
—Luke 22:51

WHEN SOMEONE CHALLENGES MY FAITH, HOW DO I RESPOND?

Devo - Purpose - Puzzle
NGA - Stunt - Jade Jackson
comes - I dig up bad
grass - Jack re-edges
most of lawn - Ann works outside -
Go to Wild Oats for cereal -
Ken Joplin works next door &
comes over - Go to circle meet at
Church - sit with Furguns - little Jane
& 'Kate' comes - Ask speaker about Ann
wanting me to go to Kenya -
- wife of speaker tells about women
succeeding in Kenya - High Country -
Aids - - S. Britton helps -
+ See Sue Thomas - House + part
of Ten Commandments -
Bank booster killed -
Bad cops on film -
Rapper killed - Eminem?

And there arose a great storm of wind, and the waves beat into the ship . . . —MARK 4:37

APRIL 12

HOW DO I KEEP MY EYES ON THE HORIZON WHEN THE WATERS OF LIFE ARE ROUGH?

Devo – Start USA puzzle – Burnet calls for golf – I par 2, 3 and 6 – 44? I shouldn't keep score – Great time with friends Charles & Walter – Home to cereal – Tiernan water for pool – dig up wild stuff in front yard – Take bags down for Ann – Talk to Howie about Hallie Young's father-in-law who has been killed – see news – Eat fish for supper – See Sue Thomas + Sniper trail – Kills of people, including friend. See Heist – – trailer member steals blue prints – some of Veronica Mars & CSI N.Y. – Superman – killed by attendant at psycho place – Football player killed by father of girl player & panicers at car wreck... Read next day of journey – Why am I here?

APRIL 13

I, if I be lifted up . . . will draw all men unto me.
—John 12:32

Is my life blessed by the gatherings of old and new friends?

Devo - Puzzle - Purpose Driven Life - Go to 1st Evan with Mulder & Matty. Home to Ann Sotilaris & Bridge on Peter. Call McCabe - Call Steve Caldwell - no answer - Do some grass chopping - Fill pool - Go get chemicals at Memphis Pool - Nap today - . Muck over for Chester. Rice - Peas - . Tomatoes + salad - Yogurt later. . See 1/2 Sue Thomas and a Musk Diss - Wig factory burns - + toupee of ugly commissioner stolen. See Preg. woman with lying mother have C-section & save baby from aids - sees 'Dead' father @ nursing home + finds sister whose letters were destroyed by Mom - - News - Logan's death an accident - Lisa Turner on T.V. - Rapist of 14 y old gets off with misdemeanor - Rosie owned by with gossip - Jack Jackson calls.

Your Father knoweth what things ye have need of, before ye ask him. —MATTHEW 6:8

APRIL 14

AM I COMMITTED TO SEEING VICTORY IN DARK TIMES?

Friday –

Puzzle - easy – Kids over to take off & clean pool cover – Get pool started – still leave oak seeds coming down – treated pool with Alkalai – Dug up & planted Nandina --- Got migraine symptoms & get nap – Have Bacon & Eggs supper – Ann goes early to get Ham and Paper @ Michael's – Mikey & Pal Garner go swimming – Give Ute Peanut butter snack – Kirstie & Nancy go shop – Kelly takes kids & get Mark Word to do some plumbing – See Close to Home and Numbers & some Mork – Crochet Dohia in Herington daughter false report case are getting off lightly – Tornado in Iowa city – University closed – Sorority house destroyed. Our Sun room air not working properly –

April 15

On the Sabbath they rested according to the commandment. —Luke 23:56 (RSV)

What can I do each day to remind me of Jesus' love?

Woke at 7 - Planned to meditate for 15-min - woke up at 9:00 - work puzzle go out to edge monkey + front lawn -- Blow back + front - Help Ann sack leaves in back. P, Rush pool - get out oak seeds - put leafy mode in garbage -- migraine yesterday - milk - see 8 Tims - went to Divine for veggie dinner - see some miracles + a number - Margie over with dish - back with flowers - Hallee back after father-in-law death - See Rose + her daughter - Read 7 day of Purpose Driven Life. No writing - nothing useful to God --

Sing . . . his praise in the congregation. . . .
—Psalm 149:1

April 16

What is the most meaningful part of my celebration of Easter?

Devo — but no 'Purpose Driven' — Vaced house this a.m. — hard work — caught sock in machine — To church with Margie & Mark — Have time in church to work puzzle — Chave — off — Home to end of puzzle — Kristie & Jeremy sleep early — She slept very late — Jeff comes to eat with Mark — Lydia & Mike were in Beaver — came late but have supper — visiting — bring food — cookies from Kristi — Ann's up congealed apple salad was great — all kinds of dessert — play some Pooh with Britt — He's going to 2nd grade at MMS — should be tested today — called Jack Jackson — get a nap as did Shu Shu & Margie — lift weights & stretch — see Crossing Jordan — un-seed part several times —

April 17

"I am with you always. . . ."
—Matthew 28:20 (RSV)

What reminders of the promise of Easter do I see in the world around me?

Up early - 7:15 - Devo - puzzle - no USA Today - machine down - Eddie picks it up in afternoon - Rake some leaves with Ann & take eight bags down to sidewalk in front - Go to Exercise - after Lunch to Dike's - See Marsha & Dad -- Talk to Bill & Marsha about eye treatment with vitamins...

Go pool top cleaning & brush bottom. Do 2 days 'Purpose Driven Life'. See News - Nap -

Mark & Marg over for left-overs. I eat no ham. Ann skips small group - Joyce sick - Marie unprepared - Dudi at IRS -

See ½ Sue Thomas - 24 hours - & 'bad' CSI Miami with Water main

For God, who commanded the light to shine out of darkness, hath shined in our hearts. . . .
—II Corinthians 4:6

APRIL 18

DO I REFLECT THE LOVE OF CHRIST TO OTHERS?

Mo USA - Devo - com, Puzz - Study Purpose Life. Go to Wild Oats & 1st TN. to give money for Kevin Jackson - Jack here - cut mulberry limbs - Clean top of jack - Thought oak seeds were done - but wrong - Take Puzzles to Steve - Amanda gives me trouble - Babe checks me for blood Pr. 2.5 - great! - Spend time waiting for Eric Johnson - Says I'm O.K. - can alter heartbeat - may put me on stress machine - Home after N - 3 hrs every nearly.. Nap - see Raymond. Eat home - & fruit salad... See ½ of Sue Thomas - to be continued. House - Live transplant - Miracles - Miss America - from short leg - Parrot gets help - woman operated on - during flight -

April 19

Pray for one another, that ye may be healed. . . .
—James 5:16

For whose physical needs can I pray today?

Up before 8 - cereal + Commercial Puzzle - pepsi + Purpose Driven Life - Clean pool - Skim + brush bottom - add shock + Chlorine - off to Exercise - Cut. Blood Pressure and trim missed spots - - short nap - - get BLT supper - see Sue Flumos - some. important Jpn. Being Ernest - + Law & Order + some miracles - Baloonflyer crashes + gets lost class ring - little girl rides bumper car for miles - off before big bumps occur - Ophelia Ford voted out - 22 yr. old kills 2's yr old girlfriend - Eat lightly - & lose sweet weight.

Nevertheless let every one of you in particular so love his wife even as himself; and the wife see that she reverence her husband. —EPHESIANS 5:33

APRIL 20

HOW DO I FEEL WHEN I LOSE SIGHT OF A LOVED ONE IN THE CROWD?

Devo - clean up Pooh - Ann off to md Pres - Muzzle - Shower & go to Church @ 1st Evan - Sit with Patty & Butler I eat salad again tonight - Mark & Marc over - see Sue Thomas & a Monk show - see 9:00 pm. Without a Trace. young men reformers - becomes pedo for child home + jailed mems - then killed in car wreck - Mournful father funds building needs - News has gang & drug arrests - kids in Mullen arrested for undercover drug swaps - Hard rain today - Keith & Al over - he sees Mom & Ann & Kate shop for basketball story purpose I think Steve has me money $150 coming from Celu - no Nap -

APRIL 21

Praying always with all prayer and supplication in the Spirit. . . . —EPHESIANS 6:18

AM I ALERT TO SIGNS AROUND ME THAT INDICATE THOSE WHO NEED MY PRAYER?

up - good night - Devot Comm. Tues 26 - Yo get car inspected - long wait - walked USA pres waiting To Mall for walk - Buy USA & go get puzzles copied - To Fresh Market for Salmon + Trip - Leave Salmon & have to return for it - Lifted weights + stretch - clean off pool - Back wash - Rains off & on - Got car cleaned in Rain

Easy to fix & eat Supper - Ann fixes fruit salad to go with Salmon - Discuss Ann's Bible study - don't get Purpose Driven done - See close to Home and Nameless - two miracles - Driver's license memorized + young boy's heart leaks to Lady's swim olympics -

Murderer dead in Jail - Watch Narnia movie L Al & Ruth in & out. Ann Ruth Barbara & Patti to Olive Branch Home visit - Bog down on Patti's Cons narrow road -

Then shall all the trees of the wood rejoice.
—Psalm 96:12

APRIL 22

HOW AM I INSPIRED BY GOD'S CREATION?

Devo - Both Books - Comm. Puzzle - Ann off to store - I stretch & walk in house 30 min. - Decide to share friendship - Call Bradshaws - Bess Ruth - Mary Jo & Boodie. See 2 History Shows - Prostitution & Freak Shows - # - News - No news - Clean up out front - & wash pool area - - Hate calls about Town - next Thursday - Dental notice - Get check from McCabe -

Ann Serves bought pork chops & Turnip Greens -

APRIL 23

Blessed be the God and Father of our Lord Jesus Christ! By his great mercy we have been born anew to a living hope through the resurrection of Jesus Christ from the dead. —I PETER 1:3 (RSV)

DO I CARRY THE MIRACLE OF EASTER WITH ME EACH DAY?

~~Work Puzzle~~ - Devo - left weights & stretch before going to 1st Evan. to hear about world over Heaven. Back house - work pool - Work USA Puzzle - no nap; but close - Ready Grill - Mark over & start fire & cook chicken - Family over for dinner - have fun -
See Crossing Jordan - & some of Grizz/Dallas game -
Dad Forrest for golf game & Merrin -
~~Jeremy~~ works on Ruth after Kristie puts in games program - Meg some - Bradshaw & Kath -

Though I walk in the midst of trouble, thou wilt revive me. . . . —PSALM 138:7

APRIL 24

WHO ARE THE FRIENDS IN MY LIFE WHO HELP ME TO ACHIEVE MY GOALS?

Devo — Ann to Dentist for root canal — I play golf with Forrest, Chas. & Walter — 40 — going into 9 — 6 & 7 —

After small migraine — ride with Forrest — fun — smoke written over it. Home to back virainer. Jack here with mulch — get 'em to dig up thinkey — Work porch — cut map — See 24. (old series) 2 hrs — news — Mark & Meg over for supper — See Sue Thomas and 24 — Some miracle & CSI Miami — Kidnapped wife in covered boat — Jack gets in luggage place — His girlfriend saved by black leader & coup — murders go on in Mps.

April 25

I have planted . . . but God gave the increase.
—I Corinthians 3:6

AM I CULTIVATING TODAY THE BLESSINGS OF TOMORROW?

Devo - 3 puzzles - Stretch - walk 30 min and lift weights - expect rain but more til night - Tornado warnings - we miss most of rain - Bartlett & Frasier - Cordova & Collierville get it. Ann brings home salmon for supper - Call Mark - Mary & Kelly about storm warnings - Second patty is thin - but large - See Sue Thomas lose dog - Herman here to juice up air conditioner - leak of some sort. Weather wipes out most of House - His dealing with faith healer. - Helps woman get well. Read Purpose - Steve calls with 2nd job to pay back loan -

The Lord is good, a refuge in times of trouble. He cares for those who trust in him.
—NAHUM 1:7 (NIV)

APRIL 26

IS THERE A CHALLENGE I AM FACING THAT I CAN MEET WITH GOD'S HELP?

Wed –

Devo – Puzzle – off to Exercise – Back to errands – Tile, Target – Dollar Tree

Work book –

Nap – call – leave Steve a message – Check yard –

Puzzle with Cena – Read from Purpose Driven life – See Some Athias + see Flowers – 2 hr. Carnegie Hall South Pacific –

Good weather tomorrow – cold & dreary today –

Gas going nuts – huge oil profits –

April 27

In every thing give thanks: for this is the will of God in Christ Jesus concerning you.
— I Thessalonians 5:18

Do I need to express gratitude for blessings which are not readily apparent to me?

Thurs—

Thurs.
Puzzle — too much —
Appeal later — Devo &
read Purpose later —
Mike over in roof &
mows grass — meals up.
Give him $60 — Go to bank —
Wild Oats — McCabe's check —
give candy there & to cashier @
Bates — Work pool — extra brush &
put in gloodie. Hope it's still good —
— See Raymond & eat ham & rice
with Mark — Marge over — See
See Thomas — catch bank robber &
crooked home repairer — To Charly
luncheon at 1st Evan.
See Monk with Mark &
lady Bank robber needed parking
space — for Bank robbery —
See Without a Trace — skating
girl disappears — with coach —
Steroids — Rapper gets 12
yrs. for shooting cop.

The fruit of the Spirit is love, joy, peace. . . .
—GALATIANS 5:22

APRIL 28

WHEN WAS A TIME THAT GIVING BROUGHT PEACE TO MY LIFE?

Devo - Read Purpose - work puzzles - No walk with Margie. After interrupted stretch with phone calls - Shipley calls - to her home @ 1:00 tomor. Work pool - Plant some Monkey grass in backside yard - See Abbey - + pet her - Looks sick - See News - Ann losing Solemn from Fresh Market - for supper - see Dolly Parton Bio + Closer to home - wife killed on her wedding nite - by former husband for money from fiance - See Numbers + some Monk - family capture - caught often in Spanish - Baby shooting victims demo Call Bratton + John Upton - Ann Glaser - try Joyce Smith

APRIL 29

Let us not become weary in doing good, for at the proper time we will reap a harvest if we do not give up. —GALATIANS 6:9 (NIV)

AM I CREATIVE WHEN I AM FACED WITH OBSTACLES?

Deco — Lift weights & stretch. Late cereal breakfast & off to Independence to Ann Burford's funeral — See Rita — James Cal & wives & children — Go to Frances' house — meet Dilma — off to early visitation & MW funeral with great singing. Take lunch home in take away baskets — Home in wind & rain & clean pool. Eat lunch & watch Grizzlies lose 3rd straight playoff with Dallas in overtime. See movies I'd seen before — Cycle wrecker — saves family at place of his accident — two orphan girls meet again after 40 yrs — Smoke detector put in at last day before fire — saves mom & daughter — win at rubbers & 5 solitaires. Bed early —

Who is like a wise man? And who knows the interpretation of a thing? . . .
—ECCLESIASTES 8:1 (NKJV)

APRIL 30

DEAR LORD, HELP ME TO BE SINCERE IN MY DEALINGS WITH OTHERS.

Devo - cereal - Get most of Sunday Puzzle Nasal - Basil - all/Vassal --
To 9:30 sermon 1st Evan - Meet woman from Covington - played Tennis with Bill Simonton - see another stunning girl - give her candy along with Pam Griffin -- Mary + Meek there - Work leaves out of Pooh -- Tar + backwash - Vaced house too -- see pitch from rough in hole for 32 yr olds 1st PGA Victory -
Mark - Marg - Mikey - Britt - Lydia Nancy / Kelly for Roast beef supper - win at Straight Bridge rubbers Read from Purpose - see some news + Home Alone + New series with small town policeman ---
More murders in Mps - LG + W fail to respond in Fraser -

May 1

And the children of Israel did eat manna forty years. . . . —Exodus 16:35

Dear God, help me to recognize Your answers to my prayers.

Devo — Stretch & lift weights before going to Exercise class. Do puzzles — read Purpose — to $100 Steve with Cem. Shut msgs — Cem to SACA group — I clean & bag leaves in back yard. See some Jayhawk in Mid-Life crisis — Dinner with Mark & Marcy. See Sue Thomas — 24 hrs — Miracles + some CSI Miami — Grizz lose 4 to straight — 12 play-off losses in row — a record. Molesting teacher out of jail contacts student she bothered — back to jail. Another teacher found with Meth + lab in back yard. Get call from Steve. Talk to David — money tomorrow — $43,000 in bank.

For you have been born again not of seed which is perishable but imperishable, that is, through the living and abiding word of God.
—I Peter 1:23 (NAS)

May 2

What steps can I take to deepen my knowledge of Scripture?

Puzzles & Dea. - Got call from Forrest - Play with Chain and Walter Hughes - Enjoy - Play poorly - Walter has one "7" on hole - (4 par) See 2 Tuesday women play ahead of us - Get 2 hugs & "play with" joke - Tempted but don't smoke - No one in club house had a cigarette. Hose to "bottom out" pool debris - Little birds pounce on Mulberry Tree - Call Frances Thigpen & Moss Simpson - See Free Thomas catch Nazi - White supremists - House (sick cop & Ph.) past 1 — And Miracles - Little girl sends balloon note to dead Daddy - Takes it by Grand - lands near Mermaid lake across country - Answers letter - sends "Little Mermaid Book - Trip to Disney World - Biting dog - One more day at home - wakes to fire saves 'em to get check at Morgan Freeman. Vote - See News

May 3

Perfect love casteth out fear. . . . —I John 4:18

WHAT FEAR IN MY LIFE MIGHT BE POINTING ME TOWARD LOVE AND COMPASSION?

Devo - Lifted weights & stretch - worked 2 puzzles - off to golf with Forrest Chas. Allen & Walter Hughes Played badly - Home to nap - to get pool tested & buy some equipment - To Ike's to check on her's sleep pills - Eat bacon sand. piece of salmon & fruit salad - lose 1½ lbs on course - See April & Sue Thomas and House - Read Purpose See Miracles - kids saved @ sea when sma. craft won't start - child fire & lungs suddenly works - woman with dog which senses her seizures - & men saved from ring of forest fire - Horses live - Rains tonite - take herb sleeping pills -

And seek the peace of the city whither I have caused you to be carried . . . and pray unto the Lord for it: for in the peace thereof shall ye have peace. —JEREMIAH 29:7

MAY 4

ARE THERE NEEDS IN MY COMMUNITY THAT GO UNRECOGNIZED?

Devo – Puzzles – Stretch – Start pooh – Ann gets back from Bible Study in time to go to 1st Evan. – Sit with Patty & Dubber. Eat only salad – scrub pooh bottom – Read Purpose – read entire Guide Post –

Worked Ann's puzzle – big rain last night – + drizzle today – Back washed pool to bring extra water down. Mark + Marge over for chicken salad – See ½ Sue Thomas and Monk CD about using Sarona's story for murder – attempt to make her think she's nuts – Munt quid's boot spur + tracks molester to boot repair store –

Teacher poisons hubby to free her for boyfriend security guard. See Without a Trace – Father flees with kids + testifys against Thugs – move to safe house –

May 5

I do remember my faults this day. . . .
—Genesis 41:9

How can I keep my focus on others' strengths?

Puzzles — Aunt Sam's
stretch - lift weights -
scrub pool — Backwash
Terri — test chemicals —
Read - Purpose & James + 1st Peter —
check front yard - Bring in garbage
cans — see needs & friends —
see Hollywood producer of Chinese
Town & Godfather — Marathon @
Paramount now — Wife was Ali McGraw —
— went with McQueen -
see Close to home — two gay boys —
one shoots other — Dad tries to take
blame — see Bank pater vanders under
Russian — & some monk —
a bit of news —

"Are not two sparrows sold for a penny? And not one of them will fall to the ground without your Father's will." —Matthew 10:29 (RSV)

May 6

WHEN HAVE I WITNESSED GOD'S CARE OF A SMALL ANIMAL?

Commerce Plaza - Devo - Luke read Purpose and 1st Peter in Eemi's new interpretation - (The Message) Stretch - ½ weights - ate lightly - moved & blew leaves

Walked with Ann & Margie this A.M. Saw Spencer Tracy in Judgment Nuremberg - Burt Lancaster - all given life -

Some news - Salmon from Sam's for Dinner - See DaVinci Inquest debunking - Some Hilda (G. Ford) & some Seabiscuit -

May 7

There are diversities of gifts, but the same Spirit.
—I Corinthians 12:4

AM I APPRECIATIVE
OF INTERESTS
THAT ARE DIFFERENT
FROM MY OWN?

Work Big puzzle after devo - + stretch - ½ weights - Bath - to 1st Evan - To Germ. Haircare for Calabrius - Do pool & vack out house. Read Purpose & enter book of Exodus - 3000 Jews die after Golden Calf incident - Aaron builds calf - scores of directions for building worship area & priest uniforms - Moses talks & men with him who repeatedly see God - news to me - Eat Pork - asparagus - corn & Pineapple. See Mystery - wife kills 3 people. Exec lives in with Jamaican woman & 2 kids Jerico - more muscles in thps Burris - calls about golf - Lois President of Chas crime club - Ruby & Lydia not here for dinner

> God's laws are perfect. They protect us,
> make us wise, and give us joy and light. . . .
> They are more desirable than gold. . . .
> —Psalm 19:7–8, 10 (TLB)

MAY 8

WHAT BLESSINGS IN MY LIFE HAVE I BEEN OVERLOOKING?

Up @ 8 - Devo - Do stretch - Cum to exercise - go to Audobon for golf with Mabry - Forrest Burris & Walter - All play terribly - learn to use Shorter Back Stroke - bath - to Dentist - see Tracey. To hair cut with Darla - She likes my old Mercedes & has moved to Brighton Home - Cum gone to sewing group - I work tough puzzle - Read entire book of Mark -- Brush pool - Marti & Marg over - tw left overs. good - See ½ Sue Thomas and 24 hrs - See Catherine the Great on Chan. 10 - Peter murdered - her hubby - a nerd - - Have murders in the english -

MAY 9

Forgetting what lies behind and reaching forward to what lies ahead, I press on toward the goal for the prize of the upward call of God in Christ Jesus. —PHILIPPIANS 3:13–14 (NAS)

DO I RECOGNIZE WHEN I'M GIVEN A NEW OPPORTUNITY TO DO GOD'S WILL?

Devo - Com. Puzz - Stretch - off to golf certi Bill Mabry - Forrest & Walter - 43 - Made me over-all winner. Home before Rain - Storm - Ann barely gets in - Back wash pooh - turn it off before storm. Read Ruth, 6 chapters of Josiah & ½ of Samuel ... Harsh treatment of the conquered — Work USA puzzle - got it all - See some of heavy water Large saboteur on 10 - some of Will Rogers Judge Priest - some of Amos & Andy film - Movie playing -

> "I, Jesus, have sent my angel to you to give you this testimony. . . ." —REVELATION 22:16 (NIV)

MAY 10

WHO WAS THE LAST "ANGEL IN DISGUISE" THAT I ENCOUNTERED?

Devo - Puzz - Stretch - lift weights - start new puzz - tries to exercise in room. 1½ miles today -

Read 2nd Samuel -- after completing 1st Samuel -- while listening to Music -
Call Monnie Rae - about Mary Jo -
Call Emily to tell Walter - no golf.
Call Burris who had bad time when work on his hand + arm -
Give David brush + Tooth paste -
Charlotte wants to know how I got run out of church - -
Notice low tire - go to Mattie's + get it fixed -- Clean front hub caps - car washed in rain - See Grand Canyon on 10 - + John Ford + John Wayne connection in movies - They did Quiet Man over Ford's protest -
Liberty Valance - Searchers - Red River - See some Miracle - Glden Run away van - + teller saved - another man shot by robber -

May 11

> All Scripture is God-breathed and is useful for teaching, rebuking, correcting and training in righteousness, so that the man of God may be thoroughly equipped for every good work.
> —II Timothy 3:16–17 (NIV)

Do I lead others by example?

Devo – 2 chapters of Purpose – walk while listening to tape of Mark – Strett – work pool – Take Hot Tub – Ann off for roof cand work – I go to 1st Evan with Patti + Mulder – meet new waitress + see old friends who work there – Bo get check + have water tested – Back home for Ann's endowment so go to bank + Kroger + Alse's for medicine shortage + back huh – Evelyn checks me out.
Bill catches candy – no key from Barbara but Bill offers Home – then go for veggies at Dixie – give candy there – at bank + Heps. "pooh"
Mark over for Sue Thomas + Monk who gets new nurse – Daughter's fish tank has moon rock
3 shows, parts of – Taliban defeat + Ben Laden's escape.

The desert shall rejoice and blossom as the rose.
—Isaiah 35:1 (NKJV)

MAY 12

DO I APPRECIATE THE BEAUTY OF ORDINARY THINGS?

Devo - 2 Puzzles - Finish reading Joseph & then Herold Goodwin's disc on Lord's Prayer - Take care of pool. & help Ann plant flowers in rock-ringed front bed - Got migraine - listen to music & rest - play a number of bridge & solitaire - Time flies - Eat pork & rice for supper - See LeGalle Blond 2 - in congress - Sally Field as power of supporter - Get sorority sisters to help get swing votes in Congress - She gives speech on duty of American leaders - Gets married 2f' hr. girl in picture - see some of Douglas Moore - Ace-pick murders - sleeps with father @ end. - See a transplant miracle - Viet orphan plane crash - Monk & "cop" killer - causes Stottlemeyer divorce - Monk & Morse -

Lifted weights & stretch

May 13

"From everyone who has been given much, much will be demanded. . . ." —Luke 12:48 (NIV)

Do I hoard or joyfully share the treasures in my life?

Devo - commenced Puzzle - slept early -- read rest of Josh --? edged the lawn + trimmed around Ann's rock gardens - Got bacon & egg dinner - saw McCrea + R. Scott in 'Ride the Wild Country' - summer wine - went to Ext's game - good pick-up @ 1st but no hit.
Met Kyle's mum - cute - witty + nice - did 'comb' trick -
Stopped at Kroger - at Sunoco + Whit Station -
Read Purpose chapter -
Read Judges - woce!

> "A woman giving birth to a child has pain because her time has come; but when her baby is born she forgets the anguish because of her joy that a child is born into the world." —John 16:21 (NIV)

May 14

Dear Lord, help me to see the joy that can accompany pain.

Long sleep @ Puzzle - after Devo - Bathe + head for K⁺ Eden - Home to lunch and edging with weed shimmer - Britt shows up and brings edger. Britt solves 2 mechanical problems - light and clears plug ground rod - I blow fuse - He's off with Grandma to find plants for Nancy's Mother's day - All family over for Sue's Mom's day dinner - Read purpose Living chapter - Kid's arrive - Mike doesn't like Britt getting grass job --- Fold up old pool cover - it's in basement...
Wash pool - leaves -
See some Mystery & Squee supposed coded org. begun by Galileo -- Bosh - See Miracle of baby eagle -
More murders - including Mills federal lady agent - crazy town.

May 15

Out of Zion, the perfection of beauty, God hath shined. —Psalm 50:2

Do I know someone whose inner beauty makes them glow?

Dev - USA puzz - Cnn to Exercise - I play Golf with Forrest - Chas Allen Walter - Bill Mabry - Shoot 42 one Bird -- Home to cereal - Read all of Acts - 1st Chap. of Romans - Win a rubber -- Solétaire - See National News - Mark & Mary over for Bar-B-Q - (mom's) + Sue's Veggies - See Sue Thomas - & 24 hrs. - delayed by Pres. Speech -- Some Miracle -- lost son - found bastard son - some old Christine -- Some News - felt good -

*Whatsoever things are lovely . . .
think on these things.* —PHILIPPIANS 4:8

MAY 16

WHERE CAN I GO THIS WEEK TO APPRECIATE THE BEAUTY OF CREATION?

Devo - USA Puzzle - Off to golf shoot 42 - Walter 43 Durrest 46 — To Wild Oats for cereal — Home to 2:00 lunch. Out to get tires pumped & gas. & Salmon for supper - orange juice - Chlorinate pool — observe Ann's plantings - call WNCC for gas info. - no good - Home to a rubber — work Cappeal Puzzle - Margie over for dinner - See - Sue - House? & some of mystery — two thieves killed by woman after they had killed judge - Read 9 chapters of Romans & Purpose - Talk to Chene. lawn...
Danny Charlie calls about aquarium clean

#

MAY 17

Heaven and earth shall pass away, but my words shall not pass away. —Matthew 24:35

When have I been inspired by someone who beat the odds?

Devo - Puzzle USA - Golf with Chas B - Forrest + Jim - O.A. + Walter play together - 47 - Chas 49 Forrest 50 - Have to cereal + Pooh - Go to bank - Mail Ann's cards - To Ike's for Ann's pills - Give candy - Sing to Delores - See Marsha who wants a million - Home to wash and wax Ann's car - WOW - See Bridge line rubber - Solitaire - Choose clothes for trip - Mary Jo calls - Ann talks to Boodie - Ask Marnie Rae about clothes - Read 2 chapters in Acts - see old vaudeville stars who made it to Radio + T.V. - Beryl Beeny Burns + Allen - Shelton - Sammie Davis Jr - Bob Hope - See Nat King Cole stories died @ 45 - smoking - See 2 miracles & get Hot Tub.
Ann to Exercise + plants out.

I have learned, in whatsoever state I am, therewith to be content. —Philippians 4:11

May 18

Am I able to be content wherever I am?

May 19

For when I am weak, then am I strong.
—II Corinthians 12:10

Am I willing to acknowledge my fears and give them to God?

Thou dost know when I sit down and when I rise up; Thou dost understand my thought from afar.
—Psalm 139:2 (NAS)

May 20

WHAT DOES GOD KNOW ABOUT ME THAT THE WORLD DOESN'T?

May 21

We should serve in newness of spirit. . . .
—Romans 7:6

How could I change my routine and freshen my perspective?

Be not wise in your own conceits. —ROMANS 12:16

MAY 22

WHEN DO I SERVE GOD MOST HUMBLY?

Left Boodie's about 9 - Eaten - Drive 7 hrs - 4004 miles - Tired + edgy - Stail pooh + left leaves - Go get food for Mark - Emi Me bee 2+ hrs. President caught by small tape abusing wife - Bauer captured by Chinese + taken to China - Prevents sub from launching missiles - see news + some CSI. Turn off pool + head for bed - Call Boodie about Katee's piano lessons -

May 23

Ask now the beasts, and they shall teach thee. . . .
—Job 12:7

DO I JOYOUSLY DISPLAY
MY PRAISE FOR GOD
OR HIDE IT
IN EMBARRASSMENT?

Devo - USA Puzzle -
Ann is treated to B.D. party by B. Lyons, B. Joplin - Nell - Marie Word &
 Go to golf with Chas & Bonnie Burris - Walter & Forrest - I shoot 42 & miss short birdie on 8 & bounce out of hole on 9 - Best in long time - Home to rest & cereal @ 2:30 -
Brush pool & test for chemicals - Stretch but miss weight lifting - Go to Marcia Cock's husband's visitation - Visit Ruth, Gil & Buddy with Ann -
--- See some Sue Thomas part 2 Confessions House - dreaming or real - His leg better - mind going? Don't know
See news of murder & police brutality & part of miracle. Call Burris - about Donnie -

Is it a small matter . . . ? —GENESIS 30:15

MAY 24

WHAT STEPS CAN I TAKE THIS WEEK TO INCREASE MY SERVICE TO OTHERS?

Several Devo's - Work USA Puzzle - Go to Britt's graduation and reception - see Sara & Mark's parents - Britt got Fantastic Friend award and pre algebra award - Kelly - Nancy - Sue - Kristie Miley - Ann & Me at Mozzam -
Go to cockeyed Camel for one free lunch with Patti - Bud - Al & Ruth - Go to
* Dollar Store for Marge picture frames & to Fresh Market for Salmon & Catfish lunch
x meet women who knows who has to be put up with - Hope to Meg attempt & call from Cadence - Balance 42,900 Visa $1600 — Call Herman for air.
Water pool - clean brush - backwash
Reat 1st Corinthians & 4 chapters of II. see some Sue Thomas. Dramatic Phoenix win over Dallas - 2 pts -
— one Miracle & piece of LUCI - N.Y.
Turn off pool water hose - then kill Pump.

May 25

But we preach Christ crucified, unto the Jews a stumbling block, and unto the Greeks foolishness.
—I Corinthians 1:23

How do I overcome the occasional stumble in my walk with God?

Devos – Puzzle – Ann to grocery – Ann goes with Ruth all afternoon. I read 2nd Cor. – Galatians & Ephesus – stretch – Go see Valerie at Bubbers & meet her daughter Hilde – Give her 2 quarters for hand – later she slaps it – Valerie's 2nd daughter dies in October. Home to Raymond & chicken salad supper with Mark – See Sue Thomas & deaf woman whose hubby abuses her & fakes his death. See Mark solve Commoner murder of his wife with fake Psycic.

See without a trace – philandering cop stops terrorist attack & dies in gunfire – girlfriend commits murder of boyfriends blackmailer –

More shootings in news –

Call unto me, and I will answer thee, and show thee great and mighty things, which thou knowest not. —JEREMIAH 33:3

MAY 26

WHEN CAN I CARVE OUT SOME ADDITIONAL TIME TO PRAY?

Devo - Puzz - To Sam's with Ann - Stretch + Lift weights - Do pool - Wash car but it won't start AAA - (Bobby here) to get me started + over to Mercedes - Ann gets me after running over golf clubs - Ruth calls twice - before + after trip to Nashville - Chlorine pool - + brush bottom eflo collecting leaves - Dinner - chick salad + soup - See Divinci Code review and Dallas victory over Phoenix - See numbers + police kill reckless driver - Oakland mayor gets extra dough $26,000 - Rocks thrown off overpass - see some close to home —

May 27

But as for me, I will look to the Lord. . . .
—Micah 7:7 (RSV)

Am I facing a new opportunity to listen for God's voice?

Worked Appeal puzz. Did Devo - Later read Ephesians and Phillipians - Got out + mowed front lawn in sweltering heat. had to lie down - Didn't blow n do back yard - I have no car. Ann went to give for a Jewish cake - 2 groceries + Sherman - I rest - nap? - do pool - Get in pool 1st after cutting lawn - a bit of bridge v solitaire - Get bacon + egg supper - see 70 most popular Country TV series. - Andy G. #1 - Hillbillies - Walter Brennan up there - with Dukes of Hozark + Hee Haw - Hot Tub -

As for God, his way is perfect. . . .
—II Samuel 22:31

May 28

Do I remember a time when I was amazed by God's solution to a problem?

Puzzle - lifted weights - some stretch - To church - give candy -- Home to Guideposts & cereal - some Solitaire & Bridge - coffee - Puzzle with Ann - Got ready for cookout - tried to help young robin - Read from Message 3 Johns - Mark over to help cook - Steak for Ann & Nancy's B.D. party - cake - ice cream strawberries - work puzzle while Dallas beads Phoenix - News - another killing. Mike & Lydia don't eat - Got shorts wet on divin, 1st. Jeremy, Mitt & Kristi swim - Sleep out house air conditioned finally -

Sermon on John 5 -

May 29

And I heard a voice from heaven saying unto me, Write, Blessed are the dead which die in the Lord. . . . —Revelation 14:13

How am I comforted by the memory of a loved one?

Devo - Appleal put - Go get car - cost over $700 - new alternator - battery & cables - Do pool - walk with Margie & Cem - See Push & Faith - and the Longest Day - Audra - Wayne Star to Robert Mitchum - - Red Buttons - Frankie Colbert - & many others - Fonda - Women given baby aeeteg fu drugs - - Sleepy Scene - Driver goes to sleep Kills man - wrecks station - no ticket - Margie here most of day & fu Supper with meal - Call BH about Saipan invasion - Richard Widmark - Do Stretch -

> "Can you bring forth the constellations in their seasons or lead out the Bear with its cubs?"
> —Job 38:32 (NIV)

May 30

When am I most keenly aware of the power of God's Creation?

Devo. Stretch - Golf with G.H. - Forrest & Burris. Shot 43 - beat everyone - par 3 times on (4-5-&8-) Home wearily after Wild Oats - got drugs on way to course. Go to Stern's - Memphis Pool - water O.K. & get some gas - Home to try finish new puzzle - Girls glad to see me @ Sterns - Help Ann get back door open & she tightens screen - rest -- Ann writes letter to Queen - We have fish & fruit for supper. See some Sue Thomas + 2 hour Aids program - More killings in Memphis - Baby traded for drugs - missing 4 days - Walked with Ann & saw Abbey & her owner —

May 31

All were amazed and perplexed, saying to one another, "What does this mean?"
—Acts 2:12 (RSV)

WHEN DID LISTENING TO AN OPPOSING VIEWPOINT ENRICH MY KNOWLEDGE?

Devo - Puzzle - Off to Golf with Walter + O.N. (who played alone) Forrest Charlie + Donnie - Shot 42 -- on grass - shredder greens - par 4-5-8 - could have paned 1st 2 - missed short putts - Home to pool - cereal - Puzz. with Ann who goes to exercise and Sarah Odams - Super bowl - + boys card - Rain comes well in 2 spurts --
Rest - short nap - meeoos + mushroom sandwich dinner - Read 12 chapters of John + see 2 hour aids show - Bush got out aids money - Horrible plague + no vaccine. Transmit sexually - drug needles + birth -

Underneath are the everlasting arms....
—Deuteronomy 33:27

June 1

With a deepened trust in God, what new goals would I set?

Devo - Puzz. start - Start Pool - off to golf with Walter & Burris - don't play too well - Home to cereal + naps - Ruth calls from Phi Delt Fraternity house - - got in pool after golf - see Candy - Work old Commercial puzzle - No Bible today - go to Rossella Allison visitation - see Blakes + Jay Wright - Jim & Mary - meet adopted offspring. Go get Hamburger - Mark over for dinner - see most of Sue Thomas - Mark + the Cobra - Jewel thief has swag in casket - Dallas over Phoenix - see some Sodom + Gomorra excavations - + some Without a trace - lost baby turns up in Milwaukee - Mary a headache.

June 2

> Who can understand his errors? Cleanse thou me from secret faults. —Psalm 19:12

AM I ABLE TO LAUGH AT MYSELF WHEN I MAKE A MISTAKE?

Devo - Puzzles - no golf - one little sprinkle. Nape (2) - Do to Dr. Berry. Get Ann's money from Morgan to bank - Sears - Get edger twine - car wash/wax, etc. To Fresh Market - Got 2 salmons for price of one - Tip $5 thru to cashier -- offer body guard service to 2 women. Teary tall cashier.

Home to puzz. with Ann & coffee before - Mid-town Shopping - got top soil @ Dan West.

Mary over - salmon on potatoes - tomatoes - pineapple. See - numbers some old music. Close to Home.

Talk to kid at Berry's - News - & to bed.

Get Keegan to send out check. Talk to Walter - Boris & Torrey. Call bank for money total 42¹ - 1700¹ - 1100

The sovereign Lord will wipe away the tears from all faces.... —Isaiah 25:8 (NIV)

JUNE 3

HOW HAS GOD COMFORTED ME IN TIMES OF GRIEF?

Devo -- Ann + Kelly to Sam's - way to p of car - Mow lawn.

Bacon & Egg supper -

JUNE 4

He has clothed me with garments of salvation....
—Isaiah 61:10 (NIV)

DOES MY OUTWARD APPEARANCE REFLECT WHO I AM INSIDE?

Deo - Puzzle - Coff & 15" Even - - - some vack - in Ketchen + Den. 1545 oven for out-door grill Pork Chops - Mark helps -

How can I repay the Lord for all his goodness to me? —Psalm 116:12 (NIV)

JUNE 5

WHEN HAVE I WITNESSED GOD'S FLAWLESS TIMING?

Dev - Puzzles
Golf with Barries - Forrest Walter & OA. - Birdie #7 - (44) double 9 - Home by Ike's with drugs - Get in pool - check it - & later brush it - Some Bridge + solitaire - Read ½ of Genesis - Eat pork chops with Mark - Margie over too - - See some Sue Thomas & Jackie Chan -
Tv CSI New York - enraged husband - kills wife - after necklace stolen by drunk - by - woman.
Kristie & Britt over for disc

June 6

> But God hath revealed them unto us. . . .
> —I Corinthians 2:10

AM I QUICK TO OFFER HELP TO MY NEIGHBOR?

Devo. Walk w/the Mackenzie C
Ann - See Abbey - Walk 450
Puzzle & off to golf w/ 1500 ts
Charlie & Walter who doesn't feel good
& leaves early — my only par on 9 —
w/the Mulligan - nice day -
Home to cereal & rest - wipe algae
off pool sides & brush bottom -
win a rudder & some solitaire - Read
rest of Genesis. Go to Art's when alarm
goes off - talk to lady Walker -
— Start Jeurticas — Read an hour
of Ben Hellfer. —
Pork chop & fruit salad
supper - Ann calls Herman &
Katherine Eddins - she seems better than
reported -

If I take the wings of the morning, and dwell in the uttermost parts of the sea; Even there shall thy hand lead me, and thy right hand shall hold me.
—Psalm 139:9–10

JUNE 7

HOW CAN I FIND MY WAY BACK TO A STRONGER RELATIONSHIP WITH GOD?

Puzz + Deco — Stretch — Golf with Harvest. Walter + Barrie — 49 — Home to pool — Nap — cereal — Puzz. with Clem — listen to 1 + 2 Thess — 1 & 2 Timothy + Titus on disc — Eat veggie dinner — Eggplants — Linies — Sw. Potato — salad — See old Sue Thomas — a 1½ hr. Gershwin life story + compositions — Porgie + Bess — some Jazz with Dave Brubeck + Davis — Talk to Betty — Try Bradshaws + left Tape — Read some Bonhoffer —

JUNE 8

Faith cometh by hearing, and hearing by the word of God. —ROMANS 10:17

DO I ASK GOD FOR PROOF TO REINFORCE MY FAITH?

Devo - Puzzles -
Off to golf with OA - Walter Burns & Forrest.
46 - Home to nap + cereal
Work pooh - See News. Al Qaida leader killed by U.S. bombs -
Marcie & Mark bring dinner.
See Pride + Prejudice - Rented disc.
Dallas over Heat in game one -
Read from Bonhoeffer &
1 & 2 Thes. - Titus - Philemon
Read in Mornings - Call Bradshaw not home - call David Reeves - no return -

You will be blessed when you come in and blessed when you go out. —DEUTERONOMY 28:6 (NIV)

JUNE 9

AM I WILLING TO RELAX AND ACCEPT GOD'S GRACE IN TIMES OF STRESS?

Puzzle - one letter off - We walk with Margie - Go with Ann to Ike's Home place - + Super Low - Nap + backpack - See some Raymond + eat Margie's la Sauce - - - D. Vinci - part of Close to Home and DaVinci - - News on Fed Ex Forum - Puzzle with Ann - Margie here most of day - Can't remember Bible subject on History Channel - Get Hair cut + go to Mrs. Pooh - when can't find Leslie's - get $7 saving - get Chlorine - Shock + free Clarifier -

* Cathedral building - St. Peters + - Glass church in California -

June 10

And God blessed the seventh day and made it holy, because on it he rested from all the work of creating. . . . —Genesis 2:3 (NIV)

Do I allow time in my schedule for needed rejuvenation?

No Britt - Mowed Lawn - swam - worked pool walls - Ann to store for broccoli - stretch & lift weights - puzzle with Ann - nap - Eat bacon-Fr. Toast with 2 eggs - see Welk show & read from.. Bonhoeffer - see Summer wind & As Time Goes By - Newson Fed Ex - mess by city - Mary, Ann & I walk early - after I cut grass - no Ebbey - Ann visits neighbor - Morton - I go see Henry - wife & Henry's pretty blond daughter.

Very Hot - 93 - today - Britt in Soccer Tourney -

The Lord is faithful to all his promises and loving toward all he has made. —Psalm 145:13

June 11

Following the Lord's example, do I honor my promises to others?

Cereal & Devo - Start & finish Puzzle minus one word - IV - Intervenous? - Brunette in Church to have her baby Tuesday - Start pool & no one goes in it - Acep - read Pleetum & Hebrews & Bonhoffer - Vic/y/oon - Solitare, Bridge & puzzle - Kids over - Have Ham & veggies - Eat lightly - See some of Dallas romp over Miami - See 2 miracles - Girl with premonitions knows about Kevin & Beth problem & wants to see their pictures of which no one had told her - Balloons sent up at her B'day party - Land by babies grave site

June 12

Lie not one to another, seeing that ye have put off the old man with his deeds; And have put on the new man, which is renewed in knowledge after the image of him that created him.
—Colossians 3:9–10

HOW CAN I CONTINUALLY SEEK TO RECOGNIZE AND RECTIFY LIES IN MY EVERYDAY LIFE?

Devo. Puzzle - walk with Ann & Mary in Pooe - They off to exercise & I edge front with Nancy's edger she brought with Brith, who was ill today -

Brush & chlorine pool - blow grass + back it - Ann off to small group - I nap - then stretch + lift weights - win 2 rubbers on bridge T.V. See news at five - call from Burds about golf. Jackson to come in morning - golf at 10:30 ✓

Eat leftovers - little ham but lots of fruit salad. See Sue Thomas and Closer. Then CSI Miami - girlfriend does one murder of wife - for white supremist - News about Jed & Jomin - wife who killed minister hubby - OJ miss knocked out of Current World S. by Miami -

Believe in the light. . . . —John 12:36

June 13

WHEN I AM FACED WITH DARKNESS, DO I TURN TO THE LIGHT OF GOD?

Devo + Puzzler - Jack + aide show up to work on pool - Golf with Burris + Hughes - We all play lousy.. To Oylers with tile - Try to call @ sleeps - Bill died in sleep — Ham sandwich + salad last dinner -

June 14

Thou has given a banner to them that fear thee.... —Psalm 60:4

How can I contribute to the nation's spiritual health?

Devo & Puzzler – Jack here working on Pooh – His aide came later – Off to exercise with Ken & Marg – Cereal – Read 40 chapters of Isaiah – written – 2nd & third part by other authors 200 yrs. apart   600 AD for Isaiah. – Assyrians retreat from Plague to Jerusalem – God's will – King giving visitive at Tour of Temple rules which they will later later – – doze off some – Eat delivered meal Schrum's – chicken pot pie – See 3 hr movie Glenn – Wonderful Life · #1 – Mockingbird 2 or 3 – Clueless being robbed – Lesbians shot at – twins born in Cal. stuck together – no golf   Rinse & wipe off car –

Thou art a God ready to pardon, gracious and merciful. . . . —NEHEMIAH 9:17

JUNE 15

WHEN WAS A TIME THAT I FELT GOD'S GRACE TOWARDS ME?

Devo - Read chapter in Narnia - walk puzzles with Ceen - Backwash after (later) brushing pooh - eat late breakfast & off to Lowe's with Ceen - get stand up fan and edger - lift weights & stretch while news goes on - Shepherd's Pie with Marli - Margie over - see Sue Thomas & Tracy with her job - & Miami ahead of Dallas by 20 in 3rd quarter - to bed because of 8:30 golf game with Burris & Walter Hughes -
Take Ambien -

June 16

Open his eyes, that he may see....
—II Kings 6:17

What moments of beauty did I witness this week?

Up early - for golf @ 8:30 with Burris - Hughes & C. Cellen - Walter plays well - but we don't.. Home to puzzles - + rest + short nap - No Jackson today - did call him - Yard treater by to check yard.

Solitaire + Bridge - eat ham + noodle concoction - Ann + Margie walk early - spill coke in legs + shorts - See. Higgens Clark mystery of Hosp. murders - wife guilty too - Married for money to later separate but 2 Drs. envolved with nurse - who is later killed -

See some coded history of Bible predictions and members where a school director kill gang member + starts war on gangs -

See news - + some item who had comments — N. Korea has long range missile

> "The swift of foot shall not . . . deliver himself."
> —Amos 2:15 (NKJV)

June 17

What steps can I take to cultivate more patience?

Walked with Mary + Ann - meet new puppy - Abbey (?) at Bubber's neighbors. Stretch + lift weights - work crummerund muscle + another with Ann - brush pool after filling + starting up. - Rain most of day + breezy around dark - lightning - supposed to rain more tonight - see some of Lady + Tramp - Whitney Seccendle + some Mac uckerera - some Thin Man - 4 star stupid - done in 1934 -

Read some Bonhoeffer and Warnie - - Pray more -

Eat fried eggplant, beans + spinach supper - good - help Ann clean up kitchen -

June 18

I thank my God every time I remember you.
—Philippians 1:3 (NIV)

What simple gesture can I make to help ease another's pain?

Devo + Puzzle before Maggie shows up & walk with us - No Debbie - To Exercise - David Kid + get Bontiffer book - Then to Ike's for unready perscription - Get lens replaced that I lost in car + didn't miss it till leaving exercise - Cereal lunch - short meditation nap - then off to Ike's for perscript. - and got her car filled up for $50 -

Home to coffee - Ann leaves for small group - Marie calls + Krista comes by to use computer for a few minutes - Jack paints file + leaves - see Read from Guide Post - + news - Eat early as Mark has meeting - See Sue Thomas as she is hired by Reading Lips - See Closer - Get confession from Killer after telling him he will die - Mother in law poisons wife of hubby - Lady lead intros boy friend to mom -

"You are my Son; today I have become your Father." —Hebrews 1:5 (NIV)

JUNE 19

LORD, HELP ME TO RENEW MY PRIDE IN A LOVED ONE.

Devo - Puzzle - walk with Margie - some bridge + solitair - Read James in the MESSAGE - check pool - Call Jack - eat cereal + dump - Go to store for Ann - get salmon for supper - plus milk + even soil @ H. Depot. Eat early - See Sue get into 2 messes - saves Jack + Dog saves her + is wounded -- See Iraq cover up to war on Frontline -- see Miracle drowned man - Cancerous boy who leaves Canadian coins - Blind horse with cataracts saved - See Miami come back to lead Dallas - Quarter + to go when I head for bed - See some of Big Sleep - end on Mr. Smith Goes to Washington for filebuster - News - and Hooks indicted - girl hijacked + kidnapped -

June 20

Thou has put gladness in my heart. . . .
—Psalm 4:7

Are my fond memories the point of departure for new adventures?

Devo – Do most of Puzzle before Mary gets here to walk – eat before walk they go to exercise – I play golf with Walter – Burris & Forrest – Shoot par thru 6 – Boggie #1 & Bird #4 – (40) Home to brush pool – get in – Solitaire & Bridge – Puzzle with Ann – nap – coffee – Write poem about Mary & Steve's kids – see part of Sue Thomas – Read some Prevention – see Miracles & most of CSI Miami – suicidal wife tries to frame men – around, drug using hubby for her murder –

Call Burris – no golf tomorrow – see some news after big dump –

For with thee is the fountain of life: in thy light shall we see light. —Psalm 36:9

June 21

DO I FIND REMEMBERED JOY WHEN SHARING WITH THE CHILDREN IN MY LIFE?

Jedo & Pazzle -- Ann to luncheon @ Perkins with Ind Pres. group .. I cut lawn edge with new edger & blew walk & lawn - sweat lots - No nap - Solitaire & Bridge leave to use computer to solve Puzzle - Vac. pool - Ann helps me get started - quite an improvement - Paint paled by rain water - Hope it improves & Brush spots in pool & hit hard with Chlorine - See some news - Mark & Marge over - We see Sue Thomas and a Monk disc - Traric Jam & two murders - dump truck envolved - See some History of Atlantis Easter Island - underwater Temple in Japan - Miracle - 911 operator give instructions to save baby - same address as her lost child -- Forrest & Burris call. - See a bit of torture & truce - about gangs. Police car hit runaway driver -

June 22 - 21

> *So we, being many, are one body in Christ, and every one members one of another.*
> —Romans 12:5

For what friends in my life do I feel especially grateful?

Walked - Prayed
Great golf - 40 -
Par thru 6 holes -
Ham + Cheese supper
Then Bogie - Bogie - Double
Puzzles -

"Who has gathered up the wind in the hollow of his hands? . . ." —Proverbs 30:4 (NIV)

JUNE 23

GOD, HELP ME TO RECOGNIZE YOUR INFLUENCE IN MY LIFE.

Devo & puzzle - walk with Ann & Margie - Golf called off because of slight rain - Stretched & lifted weights - Typed poem to Steph - Kate & Jake - Read Revelations from Menage - and Jude - look at Barkley's commentary - worked pooh a bit - Sues 5 news on chan. 7 - - Ate last night's meal again & drank juice - Nap - 2 cereal meals - Ann goes to Home Depot & Fresh Market - cake & orange juice - Walter calls - - Ann Frasure dies today - See some of Rogers & Softie others - See some Closer - wife takes imprisonment & murders - Some Monk and the Kalin astronaut - - Some members on card sharks - Prof. was big instructor provides info - to students - 2 killed & one in prison -

June 24

> And what is the exceeding greatness of his power to us-ward who believe, according to the working of his mighty power. —Ephesians 1:19

When have I seen the Lord's power at work?

Up 7:30 - Nap working difficult Commercial Puzzle - Ann to store & Home Depot for zinnias - I go back for 4 zinnias and can of Diesel which I leave at station - return for it and poison driveway crack weeds - Transplant some sidewalk zoysia to add grass place - Dig up fern - take it to back & plant it -- Cereal - nap - coffee - Read Bonhoeffer - intro + - 15' chapter Have chicken pot roast & green beans for supper -- Listen to disc of 1st & 2nd Thess. 1st & second Timothy & Titus Start 1 Peter - nap off - see 1/2 of CSI Miami - and Summer Wine pole vaulter - some weather -

Take ye from among you an offering unto the Lord: whosoever is of a willing heart, let him bring it. . . . —EXODUS 35:5

JUNE 25

WHAT GIFTS CAN I BRING TO GOD?

Check out Emmies - TV Book + Start puzzle - eat cereal shirt bath + off to 1st Evan Go to Home Depot after Church with Ann to get another zinnia - Lift weights - Stretch + Vack House while Ann goes to Sams + Store for groceries - Sermon on the danger of "talk" - Ate cereal lunch - Puzzle w/ Ann - Kids over late for Chicken - Broc - Salad - Potatoes + Sweet Tatur Patties - see Miss Marple Mystery - Wife of bishop asks him to cover-up his wife's murders - she re-visits + kills - He marries + nutty wife kills her - mystery house where girl's body is behind fireplace -

June 26

*When the Lord restores the fortunes of his people,
Jacob shall rejoice, Israel shall be glad.*
—Psalm 14:7 (RSV)

HOW HAVE I BEEN BLESSED BY THE KINDNESS OF STRANGERS?

Golf 8:30 with Burris & Walter - Forrest shows up @ 10:15 - Play poorly & well - very tired - Get in pool & scrape brown algae off sides -- Rest but no nap - Ann goes off for dinner @ Nells - Back in time to serve Mark & Sue lunch - See Sue Thomas - Walk parade (almost) See some of Brave loss to Yanks.. + History channel & later study of loss of French fleet in Egypt. Talk to Burris - Sleep at 9 - Mary helps Ann get house ready & runs errands - Kill bedroom bug - Take sleep pill - call drugstore - no fills completed -

A friend loves at all times....
—Proverbs 17:17 (NIV)

JUNE 27

WHEN I CONSIDER MY BEST FRIENDS, IS JESUS' NAME ON THE LIST?

Blow back deck for Ann + pick up debris. Off to golf with Bierris - Forrest + Walter. Shoot 40 - pay off old golf registration debt of $11.00 - Shoot 40 - beat everyone - Rode with Forrest who plays well. Home - in pooh - - meet Ann's guests for Betty Lyons B.D. party - Go with Margie to Elle's - get lens inserted + pick up needed prescription - work puzzles + have early dinner - Had lunch with Margie at her place - bought stuff at Wild Oats - See Sue Thomas got Miles re-instated - + keeps his job - Read Bonhoeffer + some weight lifting - 86 murders in Mps. already this year - Mostly young people - Mayor has no ans. to interview request

June 28

Your beauty should not come from outward adornment. . . . Instead, it should be that of your inner self, the unfading beauty of a gentle and quiet spirit. . . . —1 Peter 3:3–4 (NIV)

Am I able to look beyond a person's appearance and consider their spirit?

Devo - & Puzzles -
Start Pooh -
Golf with Forrest - see Jim
Donnie & Barnes -
Jim & over par -
Home to pool & dress for lunch at
Cookeyed Camel - good waitress -
veggie plates - Then Home - Pattie
leaves - Babber awhile - Ruth &
Al take naps - as do I -
    Margie over for Happy Birthday
song - Need Margie home with
old Elec. Razon for Mark -
    Eat chicken salad & asparagus
Mousse - See Sue Thomas - Read
Bonhoeffer - song Moses - Margie heads
for home - I imp sting with lawyer
among them -

"He goes on ahead of them, and his sheep follow him because they know his voice."
—John 10:4 (NIV)

June 29

How do I recognize God's voice in the midst of distractions?

Get up & eat cereal & cut front yard – Went to Steve's & Myts Pool – Ev yellow algae fighter doesn't seem to be working – Go to Bubber's & have words with caustic Al – no nap – Read Baseball Stories – Mark & Mary over late – See most of Sue Thomas – Mark in Las Vegas – & without a Trace – Eaten shoots self – Teacher trying to help abused son – Two Olive Branch policemen shot – one may die – Woman good for neighborhood run over 3 times & killed – Dres. ✓ Jap. Superior here tomorrow – Brush pool & sides –

June 30

A man's pride will bring him low, But a humble spirit will obtain honor. —Proverbs 29:23 (NAS)

Would abandoning my pride help me to enjoy new activities?

Devo - & Puzzle - Blew yard & vacked Pooh - Called David who is moving today & State Farm over $100 deduct refund - took it to Bank - called Boozie & Mary Morgan - no return. After Ann & I packaged framed poem to them - no walk - stretch or weights - Read considerable part of Bonhoeffer's price of Christianity - Saw - Monk & Close to Home (split) & Monk @ Dentist & numbers - Running student robs under different names. President Bush here with Japanese P.M. - visit Elvis' home & Rendezvous -

When they walk through the Valley of Weeping it will become a place of springs where pools of blessing and refreshment collect after rains!
—Psalm 84:6 (TLB)

July 1

Dear Lord, please help me to replace the pain of sorrow with the joy of Your love.

Devo - Edged & Trimmed yard - with faulty weed & no string look - Got in pool - Pool looks great - went to P.O. to mail poem to Mary's kids - wash off hood & dry - This Time - Had nap while Ann was a Sarah Adams - went thru discs & found great new Ray Conniff collections - Saw news - watered pool & fixed bath - Ann to Store - with Kelly to Sam's - See some of Kleenin in the jungle - See Kennedy tragedies - & Oswalt assassination - no conspiracy Johnson thought there was one -

July 2

. . . add to your faith goodness; and to goodness, knowledge; and to knowledge, self-control; and to self-control, perseverance; and to perseverance, godliness; and to godliness, brotherly kindness; and to brotherly kindness, love. —II Peter 1:5–7 (NIV)

What actions can I take this week to continue to cultivate my relationship with Christ?

Frailies - TV program. Big Puzzle - Hot tub & to 1st Evam - To Kroger for escaloped potatoes - Home to cereal & man - Vack floors - work pool - clean out Bar B Q grill - read chapter in Bontrager - show kids (Josh) - how to jitterbug - to Ray Coniff - check yard - grill water Marl - Puzzle - see a Miracle & part of Crossing Jordan - over eat - Mary's B.D. party - see news - Hot today - and tomorrow

Teach me wisdom in my secret heart.
—Psalm 51:6 (RSV)

JULY 3

WHEN I ENCOUNTER FEAR, WHAT CAN I DO TO SEEK GOD'S WISDOM?

Big Puzzle - off to exercise - Home to Kroger & Dollar Store - Cereal - puzz. with Ann - Water flowers front and back - move junk - Must - Jeremy, Josh & Britt play golf - Mark & Mary over for supper Ann & Margie make Potato Salad - See Sue Thomas get slave trader - watch Monk & wig stripper - whose faced with publicity & re-hiring Monk Turn on lights outside & in pool - Read most of baseball book - 2 petties - watch bedroom T.V. Kelly & Susie start cooking - Ann gets out of small group - some Bridge & Solitaire -

July 4

How good and pleasant it is when brothers live together in unity! —Psalm 133:1 (NIV)

What can I do in my neighborhood or workplace to celebrate America's diversity?

Devo - 2 commercial puzzles - Blow front yard - Ged edging gloves clear - Blow back patio + sweep drain area
Set in pool to cool off -
Eat cereal twice -
Kelly & Nancy have friends Charlotte & David with Bar-B-Q. Good desserts - see several Monk shows - I'd seen before - plus end of Law & Order -
Josh leading for Germany tomorrow - Lydia leave to Fireworks -
Read chapter of Bonhoeffer -

How great are his signs! And how mighty are his wonders! . . . —DANIEL 4:3

JULY 5

WHAT ASPECTS OF GOD'S HANDIWORK MOST THRILL MY SOUL?

Devo catch-ups - Puzzle - Sore neck - Take 2 Hot tubs - + use Ben Gay - Kelly - Nancy - Fred - Kristin over to see France beat S. America 1-0 in World Soccer - Do pool - Ho to Morgan-Keegan for Ann's check - Mention school job seek to Kelly - Go to Bank - Talk to Mgr. about loan - + to Ike's to get glasses adjusted - Oive. Puzzle - Some Bridge + Solitaire - Read 3 chapters of Bonhoeffer - see some news - eat Bar B Q sandwich with Gui's dessert concoction fu dessert - See Sue Thomas - wife helps kill hubby fu Bank Truck heist - caught digging up dough - See Ben Franklin's inventions + take notes - lift weights - String my teeth - To bed early.

July 6

Angels came and ministered unto him.
—Matthew 4:11

LORD, HELP ME TO SEE WAYS THAT I CAN MINISTER TO SOMEONE THIS WEEK.

Devo — USA puzzle —
Call from Burris Holf
with him & Walter — we
all are bad —
Home to late cereal — Kristie over &
teach swimming — Down to Bosen's
about meeting — can't find neighbors —
— try map — can't drop off
Kelly Nancy Britt over —
— Do commercial Puzzle — win
Outer Rubber — + Solitaire —
— Puzzle with Gwen — see news
— Down Street — call Rita Herrin —
Mark talks to him later — at length —
He wants to be full-time FEMA —
See Sue Thomas — catch Terrorist
Necess. men's sec. gives out secrets —
causes a death —
   Monk — has Amnesia — solves local
case — woman claims he's her hubby —
Monk on July —
   Drives 'em nuts —

Day to day pours forth speech, And night to night reveals knowledge. —Psalm 19:2 (NAS)

July 7

> How often do I take a moment to contemplate the stars in the sky?

Puzzle - Golf at 10:30 start & check pack - Burris - Forrest - & Walter - par 1-2 & 5 goofed up 3 - should had 2 more pars - 4 & 5 - Home to cereal - Lift weights - Kristie & swim lessons - Eyes bother me -- see News - lift weights - See Psyce - Dad does murders - son takes kidnapping for 5 million - Dad kills both - one by accident - 1½ hrs.

July 8

> There is a time for everything . . .
> a time to be born and a time to die. . . .
> —Ecclesiastes 3:1–2 (NIV)

How do I pass on the legacy of departed loved ones?

Devo — Aunt Green — soltaire + Bridge — check + start pool — Get ready + go to 1st Evan. for Sr. lunch — good Patriotic Program — Barney F.fe — Poetess — + Singer — Veggie dinner — talk to leader's daughter about being models — may have been a mistake — sit w/ते Pati + art — + Beta Brown + wife — + Margie — Home to nap + music — (new discs) of Ray Conniff — Eat cereal for supper + 1 bread + P.B. w/ honey — Study one Bachoffer chap.. See Mrs Daletine murder solved — Kill Mexicans — to rob 'em — See Richard Thomas — as Sheriff in plains — arson — pet wolf saves 'em —

Peter opened his mouth and said: "Truly I perceive that God shows no partiality, but in every nation any one who fears him and does what is right is acceptable to him."
—Acts 10:34–35 (RSV)

July 9

AM I WILLING TO TALK— AND TO LISTEN— IN THE MIDST OF DISCORD?

Up fairly early - No devo - Funnies. TV program + get commercial puzzle done - Get in pool - short bath - To 15¢ serm. for 2nd preacher - doze off - To Smucks for milk - Home to cereal - Vac'd house before church - Lift weights + stroll. Treat low chlorine pool.. Clean out Bar B Q grill. Mask over - We cook the chicken right. Everybody pleased with food -- see part of wild Cardinal \ Astro game. — Work Ann's puzzle — Take sleep experiment drug --

July 10

Do not let any unwholesome talk come out of your mouths, but only what is helpful for building others up according to their needs, that it may benefit those who listen. —Ephesians 4:29 (NIV)

GOD, PLEASE HELP ME TO SEE MYSELF AS YOUR CHILD.

2 Devos - Puzzle - TV - Exercise - Cereal - Deck check - Kristi & Mike over for swim - lunch - Meet their Mom & 2 little ones - Read 2 chaps. of Bonhoeffer - see news - puzzle - Mark & Marg. over - See Sue Thomas & last ½ of Tom Jones + part of Oliver - Burris calls for golf.

The Lord is my shepherd; I shall not want. . . .
He leadeth me beside the still waters. . . .
I will fear no evil; for thou art with me. . . .
—Psalm 23:1–2, 4

JULY 11

HOW IS GOD LEADING ME THROUGH CHALLENGING CIRCUMSTANCES?

Devo - Puzzle - Stretch - lifted weights - off to Golf with Walt - Burns & Forrest - shoot 42 with two birdies - Checked pool chlorine - OK. Kristi over to teach swimming - Kelly takes Britt to Dentist - Solitaire - See needs local and Montreal - Water Ann's flowers & fill bird bath - Get bacon, egg supper with Pineapple - P.B./Jelly on molded bread - recover 8 iron at Audubon - see some fine things & all star game - Nationals lose in 9th - see Imposter & lies - Preacher leaves wife & 6 children, sin takes identity in Brittan - Reunion in America - Liar to be released by customs & sent to America -

July 12

You are a letter from Christ delivered by us, written not with ink but with the Spirit of the living God. . . . —II Corinthians 3:3 (RSV)

Who would appreciate a loving note from me?

Devo - Puzzle - OED to exercise - Attempt to go to Civitan -- see Norah, Dreda - Sunon - Joe - Tiffany - Harry Bill - Charlotte - Carolyn in Park lot + Ann Kenworthy -- Deeter very silent -- Home to seein party & Puzzle - do Commercial Appeal too - call Meike - get return -- coming Friday - Go to Ali's for Cim-trim & Hair cut - Solotern + Bridge - See News - Eat spaghetti - see Woody Guthrie life & part of Pirates & Van Dyke - some news - Turn off Pooh -

They will be a sign and a wonder to you and your descendants forever. —DEUTERONOMY 28:46 (NIV)

JULY 13

AM I WATCHFUL FOR THE UNSPOKEN SIGNS IN MY LIFE?

Debi + Puzzles — walk with Ann & Margie — cereal late breakfast — Apple — Blueberries & some cereal topping for lunch — Mark & Mary over for supper — See Sue Thomas + ½ of While you were sleeping .. & Without a Trace — — Israel not war in 2 fronts — Burris calls for [?] @ 10:30 — Put in light in front walk — .. Ann aching — take Ambien for [?] night.

July 14

"Man looks at the outward appearance, but the Lord looks at the heart." —I Samuel 16:7 (NIV)

How can I align my private heart with my public self?

Devo - & Puzzle - Off to golf with Chas. Forrest & Walter - 42 one bird on 4 - Hit green on 9 + 3 putt - Home to Cereal - Started mower for Mikey & cut, edges & blows - Tired & wiped out - Heat index over 100 - Clep Mikey's small leavings - get in pool - Ann to gloomy & work puzzle with her - her ankle is better -- see some Crossfire - Drew Carey - Numbers & Monk

For we are his workmanship, created in Christ Jesus for good works, which God prepared beforehand, that we should walk in them.
—Ephesians 2:10 (RSV)

July 15

HAVE I TAKEN THE OPPORTUNITY TO MEET ANOTHER'S NEED THIS WEEK?

Devo - + comm. Puzzle - Read some Bonhoeffer - wrote Tabbie & Van - Walked in Lurene listened to 1st 7 chapters of Mark - Read rest of Mark in the Message Bible - Got in pool - tested & cleaned - Colton - See Bosn's — about next Tuesday - saw some of Photo Show. - Mark here this A.M. - Getting T.V. games. 2 cereals + Rice/chicken leftovers @ supper.

July 16

"Be strong and courageous, do not fear or be dismayed. . . ." —II Chronicles 32:7 (NAS)

Where in my life do I need to take a stand?

Drugged nite - Devo + Puzzle - Breakfast + off to Christ Methodist. Home to finish puzzle - Done - Ann naps - water her flowers in front - lift weights and stretch - no walk - Same Bridge & Solitair - Good sermon on prayer --- work puzzles w/le Ann - Invite cross street neighbors to Tues - Mike --- Listen to some music - Go to Kristen + Jeremy's for Good salmon dinner -

Home to Miss Marple. See Benedict Arnold treason - Goes south will will to join British - will part of plot - Gets Washington - was going to give West Point away -

Who sings songs to a troubled heart.
—Proverbs 25:20 (NAS)

July 17

WHAT REMINDS ME OF GOD'S PRESENCE IN THE MIDST OF STRUGGLE?

Devo - Prayer + Puzzle - Off to exercise - Home & cereal - Ann off to meet - Solitude & Bridge - Water Ann's flowers - call Adam & Derrick - did booms - No meet tomorrow - Eat Kristie's leftovers. See Sue Thomas - @ Centa and Homer's Trojan war - Earthquake got Troy - No Greeks - No Helen - No Trojan Horse - Plato writes about destruction of Atlantis - which was Santorini - News - girl kidnapped -

July 18

"Keep silent, and I will teach you wisdom."
—Job 33:33 (NAS)

Am I facing a situation where the best response is silence?

Up early – Golf at 8 – shoot 41 – win – very hot. Home to puzzles & nap – stop at Wild Oats – leave ½ my purchase – return & bring grapefruit juice for Ann. Puzzle with Ann – Lift weights & stretch – see news – water the flowers – got bacon & egg supper with fruit dish – see 2 of Gue – 48 hrs & part of Van Dyke – Veronica – evidently only ½ – pretty scary stuff – Another man murdered – Kidnapped girl found in Georgia –

> "Return to Me with all your heart. . . ."
> —Joel 2:12 (NAS)

July 19

Where can I go to feel especially close to God?

Up fairly early - Puzzles & off to Exercise - Nap - Watered flowers - Read some Bonhoeffer - Saw Sue Thomas - some Celastia -- some Van Dyke - some baseball - Cardinals hit by big storm before game - some fans hurt - windows blown out - concession stands down - Cubs lose - Chlorine pooh —
Talk to Carolyn - Jack Jackson calls - here early tomorrow —
See Susie - Betsy & boyfriend - Go to see Segals - gone —
Kidnapped girl on way home from Ga. - boy in Jail —
Ruth gets to town —
Very hot - 100° —

July 20

How can I give you up . . . ? How can I surrender you . . . ? —Hosea 11:8 (NAS)

Do I need God's help to attempt a separation in my life?

Puzzle — couldn't do it — vacked — Ruth comes — go get Al & lunch with Pattie & Bubber — Take Al to hospital & Ruth leaves — They return — as Does Ott — Dallas shows with 3 boys who enjoy a long swim — everyone goes & I eat cereal — see ½ Sue Thomas — Read Bonhoffer & see 48 hrs — Kid bomber — fighting in Lebanon US Terrorists — —
Politics heat up — sevy ½ dressed receptions at Cockeyed Camel —

Though the fig tree should not blossom . . . yet I will exult in the Lord. . . . The Lord God is my strength. . . . —HABAKKUK 3:17–19 (NAS)

JULY 21

HOW CAN I DEEPEN MY TRUST IN GOD'S PERFECT TIMING?

Devo – Puzzle – Stretch & lift weights – walked with Ann this a.m. – watered her flowers
Ann & Ruth eat lunch here then go to Barber's – I finish reading "Cost of Discipleship" – Bonhoeffer – listen to music – –
Ruth complains about my bathroom use – hid up – not fleshed –
– see last of Monk at basketball + and Psyce + part of murders –

July 22

> "To the Lord I cry aloud, and he answers me from his holy hill." —Psalm 3:4

Lord, I acknowledge my pain and ask for Your help to find peace.

Stretch - Hot Tub - Water flowers - Devo. Reread last chap of COS & Discipleship Run Book - Ruth & Cel over with friend for short visit - Ontario woman - See some of Global Warming - some news - Have minute steak - Didn't eat all of it - Marcie over after trip from Fla. Haven't heard from Mark or Kelly - 'Cross street out of town next week - no party - cooler today but no rain - While St Louis & NY got wiped out - Power gone -

And every one that heareth these sayings of mine, and doeth them not, shall be likened unto a foolish man, which built his house upon the sand.
—Matthew 7:26

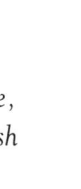

July 23

Is my life built on the foundation of faith?

Up early - Devo - Puzzle is crazy -- Got most of it - To 1st Evan. with Candy - see new mum + baby - Laura sister is pregnant - Home to cereal - stretch - lift weights - swim - get Grill ready - Listen to new disc - - Mark over to help cook - Great steak - Kelly's B.D. Gets nice presents - see odd Mrs Marple - - new lover kills Dad and Blackmailer - Women go to S. America - Another murder in Memphis - War in Lebanon causing emigree Hunger - & no place to sleep -

July 24

"He will rejoice over you in great gladness; he will love you and not accuse you."
—Zephaniah 3:17 (TLB)

How can I cultivate unconditional love for others?

Up at 8:5⁰ – Puzzle – Devo – Golf with Chuck – Forest & Walter – No pars – Mins & easy Par puts – Home to pool – Stretch – Ann off to small group – work puzzles & listen to music – water her flowers & yard spots – Mark & Marg over – See Sue Thomas after eating Steak – and a movie in the blackout – Climb 26 stories cause elevator un-even – Electricity bumbles back from dead – To save orphan murders friend –

See Same Van Dyke – and (S) Miami – both silly –

Another murder – now 100 – little girl in flasp – ars assulted & shot in head by mad man –

Judges earn over 100,000 & clerks too! Mrs Budget goes overboard from boat in lake –

He that watereth shall be watered also himself.
—Proverbs 11:25

July 25

When might I have the chance to show grace to someone?

Devo - Puzzle (most) - Off to golf - with Forrest - Charles & Walter - shoot back 9 - better - par 3 + 4 - 5 - 7 - 8 - Drive Forrest - lose 3 balls - Potty before playing (at club) Drive to Wild Oats - tease women - Home to swim - Saltern & Bridge eat cereal - No Map - Puzz. with Ann Mary Jo calls - Talk to Kelly about future - call Moreland - not home - -- Look @ Leslie sale - Go to Dic's for drinks + orange juice - candy to girls - got hug at Opti.

Didn't water Ann's plants - Visitor from Christ Meth. ---

Ann gets call from Adam NaCmi sec. Matt calls Ann - See pic of old Sue Thomas - some Gouse & Bob (Hope Facts of Life -

July 26

For it is God who works in you to will and to act according to his good purpose.
—Philippians 2:13 (NIV)

Do I set a good example in my everyday life?

Devo - Puzzles & walk up very late - Ann & Margie off to exercise - Walk w Goose - Read from Christ Methodist literature - Very good - on Christ's crucifixion & Rise from Tomb - Little rain - work puzzle with Ann - win Duter Rubler - solitaire - see CSI then N.Y. Brother in law - leaves Bro's cigarette in grave - Jane Pridgen has cancer - Need to call Tom Tyson - & Ann Askew - more shootings on news -

Let us come before his presence with thanksgiving, and make a joyful noise unto him with psalms.
—Psalm 95:2

JULY 27

ARE THERE MEMENTOS IN MY LIFE THAT REMIND ME OF GOD'S LOVE?

Devo - Puzzle - could n't finish - Read rest of Church of Christ Book - Showed it to Mark - watered flowers - did pool leaves - Went to see Deer'd Racies - met Karen - took check to Bank + cashed it - gave candy - went to work way into Dr. Dunnaway's office - got medicine from him for my head -

no nap - worked puzzle with Ann - saw news - Can buy gun quickly to keep at home -

woman who drowned 4 of her kids gets insanity sentence -

Guy who shot + raped baby girl in court in bullet-proof vest.

Mark + Mary over - Ann makes meat loaf - see part of Sue Thomas - Monk (old) + without a trace -

July 28

> For you were once darkness, but now you are light in the Lord. Live as children of light.
> —Ephesians 5:8 (NIV)

What steps can I take to brighten the lives of others?

Devos - Puzzle -- Off to vote - 1:20 - worse later - needed help - couldn't find all candidates - walked 30 min. in license - See Ben Hur on T.V. - Kelly, Brith & friend over - to swim - Kelly has made no plans to teach - or anything else - do pooh leaf work - very little rain - didn't water plants today -- see News - Monk after Bridge & Solitaire - got Bacon & egg supper - See some Psche - + a bit of Numbers - Raped girl does shooting, or has it done - Ann gets hair cut -

As it is written, "No eye has seen . . . no mind has conceived what God has prepared for those who love him." —I CORINTHIANS 2:9 (NIV)

JULY 29

WHICH ELEMENTS OF MY LIFE WOULD I WISH TO SEE IN HEAVEN?

Ann & Sam's with Kelly — Work puzzles — little rain — Ann to grocer — Help Margie with oil problem — walk with Lee — Read last chap. of Cost of Discipleship — Did lift weights & stretch — saw A River Runs Through it — sad — friend killed — Dad preacher — Fishermen in Montana — Eat meat loaf & fruit salad — Mark over to see St. Helens — & Munk in prison — see Summer Wine & end of Mex gold stealers — More shootings — 2 burned bodies in truck — Hot weather coming all week — Marks B.D. 51 —

Lost lottery

July 30

Let the word of Christ dwell in you richly. . . .
—Colossians 3:16 (RSV)

When do I feel most strongly connected to Jesus?

Bad sleep — eyes in pain. Devo + try impossible cross. Puzzle — Off to 1st Eden after Hot Tub — lunch at 9:00 — see most of Overboard with Goldie Hawn — Amnesia — a hollow life to a good one — See some of Mrs. Congeniality with Sandra + last of mystery on 10 — Cook Steak with Mark for his Birthday —
— news — Israeli Bombs kill women + children

For the word of God is living and active...
—Hebrews 4:12 (NIV)

July 31

Am I still excited when I study the Word of God?

Devo - Puzzle - rose Corner Puzz. on way to exercise - late lunch - water flowers - Rain comes - deal with pool - see last part of Thin Man - James Stewart the murder - James - Lift weights win Bridge Kiebber - call for Mity Teesie - Mark & Mary over - Mark ill - see Sue Thomas and History Ch. account of Athens with Pericles - Spartans win with plague hitting Athens - see Helen Keller story & bit of Sodom destruction - Gave in Town selling Book Heat every where - car jacking -

August 1

*Bring joy to your servant, for to you,
O Lord, I lift up my soul.* —Psalm 86:4 (NIV)

How did a challenging situation prepare me to accept joy?

Off to golf early — Beat Walter & Chas with 41 — — To Wild Oats for cereal & topping. Go to David's for check — Spend long time at Mercedes — Ellen confrontly & Susas leaves early — Hostess friendly & little pay received — Didn't fix car — but cooler — Get 2 lottery tickets — & gas for Ann — To Fresh Market for Salmon & fruit — forget Milk — no nap — swim — help Miley with lawn — — Ann gives him little money — See Sue Thomas - History — Van Dyke mega accidents & young girl on Dutch - Nape — ugly —
Meds — Oriental machine gun cop cars — & caught — Ann help & Maggie —

Like arrows in the hands of a warrior are sons born in one's youth. Blessed is the man whose quiver is full of them. . . . —PSALM 127:4–5 (NIV)

AUGUST 2

DURING BUSY TIMES, DO I REMEMBER TO THANK GOD FOR HIS ABUNDANCE?

Devo - Worked last pizz quickly - Went to exercise + store certn Aue - for Mushroom Supper - Watered Ann's flowers - no walk on grass - Do letter puzzle - call Ann Fraser + Kelly + he doesn't sound enthused about going to Miss - - -
See Sue Heckus - Lift weights + stretch - help Ann with puzzle - See CSI NY. Miss power ball - $170,000,000 I have shooting - Peeping Tom arrested - two burned shot first - Election tomorrow

August 3

I was as a beast before thee. —Psalm 73:22

AM I RECEPTIVE TO THE NEW PATHS THAT GOD SUGGESTS?

Golf with Chas & Wally Par 1 & 9 only — Home to nap — go to Gardino's to get tooth crown set. To fresh market for Roses for Dunaway's girls & Ann. Ann get boil removed & I get in to have cyst taken off back ——.
Mark & Marg over — Chicken salad & fruit salad — See Sue Thomas — Diagnosis Murder — Roma Downey on — Election returns on news — No Monk — but see end of Taped Mystery — Swim in pool —

We do not have a high priest who is unable to sympathize with our weaknesses, but we have one who has been tempted in every way, just as we are. . . . —HEBREWS 4:15 (NIV)

AUGUST 4

HOW CAN I BE MORE PATIENT WITH MY SHORTCOMINGS EVEN AS I STRIVE TO IMPROVE?

Devo + Puzzle -
Comm. Tue. later -
Solitaire + Bridge.
Get check in mail - Take it to bank - - Go to Toyota in Bermudlow for Margie - who has to leave her car 'til Saturday - Lift weights - stretch + brush pool bottom - - Buy man cue -
Ann + I work puzzle + talk about past - + poor times - to better -
No word from Kelly -
See 1/2 UFO stuff - Mork + Dr. Who lulls girlfriend + boat docker - Mork jumps ship + swims by instructions - realtor woman talks to Capt. Stallemeyer -
See Numbers + some more UFO - Kids w/ex machines+ gunned police cars had no previous records. "Kidnapped" girl walks in Police
Sta.
Call Karen + ask if David could keep
Geo Suit.

August 5

"Stand by the roads, and look, and ask for the ancient paths, where the good way is; and walk in it, and find rest for your souls. . . ."
—Jeremiah 6:16 (RSV)

Do I keep my upward focus in the midst of uncertainty?

Devo - - Aug-6 -
Go to 1st Evan luncheon & hear Harmonica players. Then to Coy Company's funeral - Get to see Haley & Coley & Mary - Roy speaks — and & me - very, very sad.

August 6

"He is not far from each one of us."
—Acts 17:27 (RSV)

Lord, thank You for Your ever-loving presence.

Stretch - Drive - Hot Tub - walked Cam. Puzzle - Off to 1st Evan - Marg + Mark - sermon too long - Home to cereal - + nap - worked on poem - no one goes in - Cath Cleaken outside with Mark - one leg race - - see Some Moore + old 'Tracy' & lesbian women - Cathy accepts - Read some Guide Posts - Kids enjoy dinner - Kelly cleans up -

August 7

He also saw a poor widow put in two very small copper coins. "I tell you the truth," he said, "this poor widow has put in more than all the others. . . . she out of her poverty put in all she had to live on." —Luke 21:2–4 (NIV)

What new opportunities do I see to share my treasure?

Devo - Puzzle - Talk Cam. D. to Exercise which Joe Bryan & leads us with Heifer's help. Water Ann's flowers & brush + backwash pool. Mark & Mary over for chicken - Sue Thomas & Merle in traffic jam -

See CSI where Judge lets murderer go - and Van Dyke finds Mayor's wife kills him -

News - stolen car + break ins Alaskan pipe line shuts down - lack of proper service -

Vac floors - for Ann

A wise man will hear, and will increase learning. . . . —PROVERBS 1:5

AUGUST 8

DO I TAKE THE TIME TO SEE THE POSITIVE ASPECTS OF EVERY SITUATION?

Golf with Ches. & Walter. Lights out at 5:30. Ann calls me idiot - Shoot 41 or 2 - beat others - Go to Wild Oats & Ole's for drugs & glass lens - Home to Ann's party for Ann Gslow - water plants & blow patio - Great party - to Bank about loan - Home to bridge & Solitair - girls Stay long time - Marie - Dolly Ryons & Norma show up for laugh time - Sue very little to eat - from 1 one piece of chicken - see part of Sue Thomas - work puzzle with Ann - See some Van Dyke, Key Largo & El Dorado. Kitchen & Come -

August 9

Gray hair is a crown of splendor....
—Proverbs 16:31 (NIV)

DO I HAVE A HEALTHY PERSPECTIVE ON AGING?

Devo - Puzzle? - Golf with Ches & Walter - beat em with 41 & 2 - Go by Super Save for milk & orange juice - lift weights & stretch - see News - & Sue Thomas - virus attack thwarted - see last of 7 Brides & part of another Jane Powell - got 2 lottery tickets but didn't get numbers - see Dick Van Dyke - new fragile - murders & sex offenders on News - another Chemical fire - 100% today & tomorrow - Furest gets dizzy -

Now no chastening for the present seemeth to be joyous. . . . —HEBREWS 12:11

AUGUST 10

WHAT LONG-TERM REWARDS COME FROM SHORT-TERM STRUGGLE?

2 Devos – after golf with Chas. & Walter –
May poorly – Chas. improves
Par # 4 with great putt –
Ann House – to store – work porch – gets windy – no rain tho' –
Read from W.K. Encyclopedia –
Walk 2 today ½ + 2 ccu. pm –
Take nap – play cam, solitaire & Bridge –
Shoulder sore –
Eat hamburger & corn with Mark
Mary over in clean car –
See some See Thomas – Grandma'
Mark disc with Mark & Margie –
Cat sneezes – Antique chair –
Kidnap –
See oriental "Without a Trace"
& baby murder on news –
Hijackers caught in London (24)
Tip from Afghanistan –

August 11

"I have been sent to speak to you and to tell you this good news." —Luke 1:19 (NIV)

What passage of Scripture do I find particularly uplifting?

Devo & Puzzler — Go to bank with Ann & sign papers — give candy — get laughs — Bring Ann home & head for Sterne's Clinic — Got P.M. (high) then up to lab — loose test there — To Ihps. pooh for water test & shock — To Am South back to get loan data closed — To haircut & over to Ike's for ocusoft — cough drops & Nyquil — Girl — Home to pooh & call from Faye (Babe) to have another check in a week — Stretch — lift weights — See news — read more from religion mag. — see Mork & Psyce —

Lord . . . you have made my lot secure. The boundary lines have fallen for me in pleasant places. . . . —Psalm 16:5–6 (NIV)

August 12

How am I blessed in ways that others are not?

Dido + Dame. Puzzle. Margie calls to cook & I don't go to Mrs. Pool for chemicals + treat pool as late as 9:00 pm. See McBride Mystery - + CSI NY. - Don't know who did murder - Run to Sam's + other grocery later - No reading today! Awful

August 13

"... For your daughter-in-law, who loves you and who is better to you than seven sons...."
—Ruth 4:15 (NIV)

IN WHAT WAYS DO I WELCOME NEWCOMERS INTO MY LIFE?

Sunday do stretch & weights after working puzzle - To 1st evening - 2 new babies - & pregnant sister ... K. Family over for swim - Mark & I cooked Pork chops Everyone liked them - saw Teacher Movie with 'Friends' star - to NYC to teach unruly children - Bed at 11:00 pm.

Every three years once came the ships of Tarshish bringing gold, and silver . . . and peacocks. And king Solomon passed all the kings of the earth in riches and wisdom. —II CHRONICLES 9:21–22

AUGUST 14

WHAT RICHES OF THE NATURAL WORLD BRING ME JOY?

Devo – Puzzle – Call Stern – supposedly sent me a postruning letter about Phone exam – No letter today – Mike over to cut lawn – gets in pool – I walk in house & stretch – Work Puzzle with Ann – get in pool after walk – Treat yeast infection – See news & some Raymond – Pill in Frank's pocket aroused Marie – see Maude's family & Hilla's building plans – Architect Speer spends 20 yrs. in prison & ends up in England – see some CSI & Van Dyke as priest – looking for tape – News about car-jacking – Mark & Marg over. Eat another Pork chop – see 'Old Christine' 'Pootie' –

August 15

Be silent before the Lord God! . . .
—Zephaniah 1:7 (RSV)

How do I feel God's presence in my moments of silence?

Left am 8:30 for Stern Clinic — Blood Test Pacer test — & see Dr Johnson — Home to 1st food + nap — Puzzles — one with Ann — Stretch & lift weights — no walk
See news (1 hr.) — 1 part of Raymond — Had gone to Wild Oats with Ann's list — got lime from young worker — wife give 2 candies — woman smiled in a flirt. Home to sight poem — Water Ann's flowers. Bob Lyons by to get Ann's arthritis treatment — see lady mystery — Mrs. ants — cucumber mussel of nurse — Cubs tied with Astros — Top of 6th — Caitlin home invasion Nurse snatched from car with 2 people inside. Big drug bust.

But he said to me, "My grace is sufficient for you, for my power is made perfect in weakness." . . .
—II Corinthians 12:9 (NIV)

AUGUST 16

GOD, HELP ME TO SEE THE POSSIBILITIES IN CHANGED PLANS.

Golf with Boots, Walter & Chas - poor games - Good company - Home to puzzles & lunch - Off to Cadence for check for Kelly - over to 1st TN. to deposit in Kelly's debt - Offer body guard help - Manger may need - "I don't guard men's bodies - Get in pool & golf - Read from Quotations Book - See news - Eat salmon I got from Fresh Market - get prescriptions at Ikes - Supper - & journeys of Bible - See Mystery woman solve murder - Uses Russian Mob contact - Gets Randy out of jail - son receives inheritance - Vislin gassed - Vaced pool - Watered Ann's flowers -

AUGUST 17

I will be glad and rejoice in thee.... —PSALM 9:2

DO I RECOGNIZE THAT JOY CAN BE FOUND CLOSE AT HAND?

Golf with Chas. & Walter 75? — Home - Ruth & Al follow me in - Work USA - eat cereal & go to bank with forms & ID's for eye drug - Then to Ott's with Ruth & Ann had eaten - Leave & Al gets here before they do Search for closed Restaurant - Lot's of memory problems. Took back washers on Alum- See news & some Raymond began Mark gets - here for Healthy Choice meals - Mary owes - Mark & I see Sam mama- gone brat - Philly Football & Mystery Woman - he sees half & I see all -
No Map -
Ott refuses my sandals

What manner of man is this, that even the winds and the sea obey him! —Matthew 8:27

AUGUST 18

HOW CAN I BE MORE GRATEFUL FOR THE CHANGES IN WEATHER THAT GOD PROVIDES?

Two Puzzles - Ruth over & Carolyn later - Go to Sterne for PT - down lower - go back next Friday - Go to Mrs. pool & then to Schnucks for Roses for girls - Get complete lab report. Home to lunch with Ruth Carolyn Sam eat piece of their cake - Treat pool - which was back-washing - Nap walk 30 min .. lift weights & stretch - Music - & see news - Eat cereal supper - see Mystery women - Western stuff - Gambler problem with Annie Oakley. piece of music + Psyche - News robbers caught .. teen girls molested -

August 19

*The righteous shall flourish like the palm tree. . . .
They shall still bring forth fruit in old age. . . .*
—Psalm 92:12, 14

WHAT UNSELFISH DEEDS BY OTHERS BLESS MY LIFE?

Devo - Come Puzz - early cereal - Stretch - walk 30 min in house. Jody & kids over to swim - they enjoyed! Ruth takes Ann to book club - she went to grocery earlier - Got migraine - + naps - See news - Eat late supper - See Mystery Woman - & late news shootings -
They spend time at Bubber's - Read final chap - of Church of Christ meth. book about proof of resurrection

Blessed are they which are called unto the marriage supper of the Lamb. . . . —REVELATION 19:9

AUGUST 20

WHAT EARTHLY ACTS REMIND ME OF GOD'S HEAVENLY PRESENCE?

Up early - Devos - Jumies TV Book & Puzzle - missed one letter - Stretch - lifted weights & walked 30 min. before hot tub & off to 1st Even - Home to cereal & nap - Start pool Watched Jane Doe & ate Taco salad with kids - some solitaire & part of Without a Trace - quit watching & Read UK. History - Vacced house for Cinn - Had good rain - wow!

AUGUST 21

And to know the love of Christ, which passeth knowledge, that ye might be filled with all the fulness of God. —EPHESIANS 3:19

DO I RECOGNIZE THE SOMETIMES-SUBTLE WAYS IN WHICH GOD SHOWS HIS LOVE?

Sleep 'til 8 - work Today Puzz. Cross. puz. on way to exercise - Home to work pool bottom - Edge grass waiting for Mikey who finished job - Stretches walk 30 min. See news - Solitair - Check on Company address - Eat Sunday dinner again w/ bro Mark. See Cary Grant as an Angel w/ Loretta Young + Niven. who died in '88 - See CSI Miami - & part of Chan. 10 uncovering mysteries of history - camera made of tin can & lens in Yankee Prison - Grace Kelly car I.D. by woman - More robberies - Lady S.S. teacher dis. missed after 60 yrs. "Cause She's a woman - Burris call. Mary ones too - Meg & I Talk sarcin -

Then the waters had overwhelmed us. . . .
—Psalm 124:4

AUGUST 22

IN TIMES OF APPARENT CHAOS, GOD, I TURN MY STRUGGLES OVER TO YOU.

Golf with Burris & Walter - By Wild Oats - get in Pool - Nap - work puzzles - Went to Kristie' volley Ball one-sided - opponents had nothing - see Nancy & Jeremy - To Schnuks - met salesewoman 3 times by chesier - eat early - see some of Egypt log book - older than Bible - see a Lt. Jane Doe - - Owner of Co. steals - Agent guilt & shot in leg - Jane in danger all the time - She & son decipher lab Top Kid gets elected - Cheer-leader sister undone by friend -
Lots more robberies - car jackes or rape -

August 23

Be honest in your estimate of yourselves, measuring your value by how much faith God has given you. —Romans 12:3 (NLT)

In what ways do I positively influence the children in my life?

Golf with Walter & Charlie — Aim to Exercise — Work Puzzle — call Forrest & Boots — Try again to get Company's — no luck yet. Brush pool — & Back wash — Walk 30 min. — small stretch before golf — See some Katrina repair — 2 hr. Jane Doe — Mobsters — ~~Daughter~~ plays well with son doing bass on computer — Makes up with hubby —

August 24

"In every way and everywhere we accept this with all gratitude." —Acts 24:3 (RSV)

Do I remember to express my gratitude to others?

Golf with Chas + Walter — Par #2 & 9 - Hit green on 9 - Birdie 1 inch short - Home - Ann gone - no alarm on. Burm -- puzzles (3) list + Commercial - map — Walk in house — weights + stretch before golf.

See news — Mark over before leaving for New Orleans —

Many calls — see news — eat mushroom & nuts for supper — see read most of Budapest — & see Jane Doe - re-run. CEO sub the villain —

Ladies clean carport.

— Stock goes up —

See Buckle and sister with Mercedes running — Big Drug Bust — Movies coming to Mps?? Big Project in Southhaven underway — Mark calls from Meridian.

August 25

Do good . . . hoping for nothing. . . . —LUKE 6:35

HOW CAN I MAKE SOMEONE HAPPY WITHOUT RECEIVING ANYTHING IN RETURN?

Devo - To Ike's + Fresh Market for 12 roses - Ann comes in from eye shop - & I give her flowers... Out to Sterne to check on Blood report + spread flowers upstairs - see Sharon Goldstein - make jokes -- Girls at Conn. du Clinic still have fresh roses from a week ago - Home to nap - no exercise - Go see Kristin volleyball team win easily -- Home to news & pool treatment - &c. Read rest of Guidepost & see Jane Doe - foil cop's bank robbery - Daughter-trouble with boy friend - son keeps find locators of Dec. of Independence - clock stopped on surveillance cameras - HS football underway

So he went down and dipped himself seven times in the Jordan . . . and his flesh was restored like the flesh of a little child, and he was clean.
—II Kings 5:14 (NAS)

AUGUST 26

IN WHAT WAYS HAVE I EXPERIENCED GOD'S HEALING IN MY LIFE?

Devo - Came. puzzle go to Ike's + Fresh Market - eat hamburger — see some Arenas & Old Face - McBride trial - good — saw of Katrina — some of cartoon Bible character take Jericho — some of Ottoman Empire — some old Egypt — Marie calls — - on way home — from N.O. - -

August 27

"Unless you change and become like little children, you will never enter the kingdom of heaven." —Matthew 18:3 (NIV)

Where in my life can gratitude replace grumbling?

Puzzle - Devo - Vack
✓ Stretch before going to
1st Evan. Home to
snack - nap & Vack book
Clean out cooler - start fire for
park leaders - mask keeps -
See Without a Trace --- kids over
except Miley & Lydia -

"It was not you who sent me here, but God. . . ."
—Genesis 45:8 (NAS)

August 28

Do I acknowledge and act upon God's nudges when I feel them?

Up at 7:30 – Devo – USA Puzz -- Do stretch off & Exercise - work com. Puzzle before lunch - Stop at Ike's & Vack store with air purifier Home - check pool - some rain - go to Sharper Image for refund on back belt & to U.T. for eye appointment - Then to Verine for Wednesday check - Home - leave car in drive for wash in rain - lift some weights - Shoulder sore - See news, local & national - Argument students fight - 3 to Hospital 23 arrested & suspended from school See Bob Hope & Hedie Lamar in favorite Spy - over film - He plays 2 roles - See end of Kristie mystery & part of Van Dyke & CSI Miami (re-run - Prez & employee married) - escape - Hurricane headed for East Fla. Talk to Brooks

AUGUST 29

I have called daily upon thee, I have stretched out my hands unto thee. —PSALM 88:9

WHEN HAVE MY PRAYERS TO GOD HELPED ME TO CAST OUT FEAR?

Devo + Puzzles - H.M. Nap Shower Sleeve - Read from Matt. in ___ ? Book Go to U.T. Med for 2 hrs to get eyes checked -- give candy - too much for nurse -- Dr. Morris. Had seen him before - Return by Walmart for milk - Brylcreme + Arm-pit spray -- Feel weird at home. eat pork again (salad - Play Bridge + Solitair - see some Veronica Van Dyke + Outer limits - Amish - Sexual abuse - Conscience favors converted sinners. - Cults - Eliz. Vargas -

Let each one do just as he has purposed in his heart; not grudgingly or under compulsion; for God loves a cheerful giver.
—II Corinthians 9:7 (NAS)

AUGUST 30

HOW CAN I INFUSE MY GENEROSITY WITH CAREFREE JOY?

Devo - Stephen Puzzle - To golf with Purvest - Walked w Charlie - 45 - min all my putts - Home & shower snack + off to see Dr. Vieron - not much help - Home & nap - - see news - fight at Oregon Inn - now at Treadwell - City schools won't comment - need Bradley - see 20/20 disasters + Bible History - Van Dyke + a bit of Without a Trace - - Armadilla invasion - crooks with 1st arrests loose in streets - Chicken salad supper - 2 help - lift weights

AUGUST 31

"I have set my rainbow in the clouds, and it will be the sign of the covenant between me and the earth." —GENESIS 9:13 (NIV)

HOW DOES GOD REASSURE ME IN TIMES OF STRUGGLE?

Devo - Puzzle - Golf with Walter + Forrest + Burris 42 - Par 4 holes - 3 in a row - one double? Walter 41 — Home to swim + lunch + off to Vernon's office with report from Stern - see nurse - no shave - got 3 pens — trade one with - Pennie... Home to wash both cars - another swim to cool off - Hear music - tired - Mark comes for chicken salad - cottage cheese + stuffed eggs - (for lunch).
 - See Miss. State lose to S. Carolina only one TD on trick play lateral pass - See some China Beach with Jane - some Trace - a some Diagnosis Murder. Meth lab found in Byhalia - Nice cool day...

For thy steadfast love is before my eyes. . . .
—Psalm 26:3 (RSV)

SEPTEMBER 1

DO I LIVE AT A PACE THAT ALLOWS ME TO NOTICE THE SMILES ALONG THE WAY?

Puzzler - call Sterne for Lipid appt - Call David's office for Ann's money - not in yet. Call Kelly to do Lawn - and he does - Read a lot from ——'s Matthew - Get Bacon Egg dinner - See the Mouse "Roar" Sellers - invades U.S.A. - Q bomb - Tidens run over Green Bay - Minn. 10 over NBA 7 - Walk with Ann + see Abbey - stretch - lift weights - Ann gets hair done + dyed - Nap for me - hear mouth organ music - - Sen. Bowers letter in JU!

SEPTEMBER 2

> *Observe the commands of the Lord your God, walking in his ways and revering him.*
> —Deuteronomy 8:6 (NIV)

WHAT GOAL MIGHT I ASK FOR GOD'S HELP IN ACHIEVING THIS WEEK?

up - puzzle & devo - walk with Ann & Marg - Ann goes to grocery twice - de-leaf pool bottom - then brush it - short nap - Read extensively from Matthew - Barkley - see Ga. Tech & part of 3 Sue Thomas stories. Tech loses 14-10 - very close & very tired - Eat chicken salad & fruit & melon melon - Yard looks great.

Listen, my beloved brethren. Has not God chosen those who are poor in the world to be rich in faith and heirs of the kingdom which he has promised to those who love him? —JAMES 2:5 (RSV)

SEPTEMBER 3

DO I PASS ON MY FAITH TO FUTURE GENERATIONS?

Devo - Start Big Sur. Puzzle + finish - Do stretch. Then off to 1st Evan - five Sunday - hear good sermon on value of today - + blessings even the poor have - ice cream in summer - Veggies in winter.
Home to Vack horese + Read Barclay's Matthew
Kids over - Miss loses to Ole Miss + Newsville kills Ky -

September 4

Remembering without ceasing your work of faith, and labour of love. . . . —I Thessalonians 1:3

God, help me to consider how I may live more positively in all areas of my life.

Labor Day - Comm.
Russ. after Serv -
Get pool going -
Still some stopping -
something wrong -
Read + complete Barclay's Matt.
Start Goodspeed's Paul.
Kelly - Nancy + Britt over to
Bar B Que - Am buys @
SuperLow - See Miami beating
Fla. State - poor play -
See CSI Miami (continued)
Some Van Dyke + some Frank
Lloyd Wright in Buffalo -
Depression wipes out
Supporter's torture + deceit -

Walked with Mary + Am.
Stretched + did weights

> "As the branch cannot bear fruit by itself, unless it abides in the vine, neither can you, unless you abide in me." —John 15:4 (RSV)

September 5

Is living a faithful life the focus of all that I do?

Devo – Walked with Ann. Did puzzles – went to David's for Ann's check. Gave flowers to Karen & Ann. Got Ann's endorsement & off to bank & Wild Oats – Nap after lunch – Read about Paul – & take Ann to Ike's for glasses & drugs – Get gas & 2 Powerball tickets – Marsha measures eyes for me. Tries couch – Home to read & News – Check pool out – Eat ribs – fruit salad – See House & Standoff – & Chan 13 news & some Van Dyke –

September 6

I prayed for this child. . . . —I Samuel 1:27 (NAS)

Do I make my life a blessing to others?

Devo + Puzzler - GGG & Exercise - Then to Super Low where we see Ken and shop for Bubber - Go by his house on way home - have deli food + nap. Lift weights + stretch - work pool - seems OK. - see News - Eat same lunch for supper - - Read Paul + Barkley's Sermon - CSI + are we safer now with Katie Couric - Bush interviewed - 2 car wrecks - one in Miss. Co. kills 2 - 75 yr old man shot at his home with own gun when robbers try to get in his tool shed. School security still poor -

The Lord hear thee in the day of trouble . . .
Send thee help from the sanctuary,
and strengthen thee out of Zion. —PSALM 20:1–2

SEPTEMBER 7

WHEN HAVE I FELT LED BY GOD TO HELP SOMEONE DURING A TRAGIC TIME?

Devo - Puzzle - Sketch & walk 20 min. in house - Hot Tub - shave - off to 15th Evan. with Ann Sit with Ott, Margie & Patty - Ask preacher about my dozing off - Home - Then to Pedologist Arnroff at 2:00 - Cause laughter @ desk about lost hair-do - One nite off to Wild Oats for pills to fight arthritis - Get stretch plans - Call Ike's about medcare - no dice Take pills - see news - some Raymond - a bit of reading - Check & back was poor - Must over for BBQ - see Robert's new show - "Til death - some Pitt - Miami game - Some without a Trace. Slalom girl - Steroids - Throws greater in period - lot of TIVO ToTo

SEPTEMBER 8

There is neither Jew nor Greek, there is neither slave nor free, there is neither male nor female; for you are all one in Christ Jesus.
—GALATIANS 3:28 (RSV)

WHAT CAN I LEARN FROM SOMEONE WHO COMES FROM A DIFFERENT BACKGROUND?

Devo + Puzzles — Golf with Chas, Jim + Forrest — Made 40 — Jim 38 — Par 3, 4, 5, 7-9 — Home to swim — lunch — Off for haircut & glasses at Ihe's — Try for map. Get Bacon & egg supper — Read Paul — See Monk in garbage strike — acct. the murders. Nothing else worth watching. Eyes Party — head for bed @ 10:00 Ani's watching news. Do some shoulder exercise. Dr. Vieron calls — says I don't need anemia med — Blood too thick — call from Sharma — increase dose —

> Bear with each other and forgive whatever grievances you may have against one another. Forgive as the Lord forgave you.
> —Colossians 3:13 (NIV)

SEPTEMBER 9

AM I WILLING TO PRAY FOR SOMEONE WHO HAS OFFENDED ME?

Ann to Sam's with Kelly. Then to grocery — A do dear + Camm. Pizz. Watch ball games — Ohio State beating Texas at big one. Ga. over S. Carolina. Miss + Miss State lose big — TN ekes out over weak team — Auburn wins — Bama barely over an arthritic S leader — left weight — stretch + walk in house 30 min... read Paul — Eyes suffer — start to go get sun glasses but she's closes at 4 — Football has evidently started too early — poor play. Ky wins over some Texas team — Louisville wins big — rank #12

September 10

For now we see through a glass, darkly; but then face to face: now I know in part; but then shall I know even as also I am known.
—I Corinthians 13:12

Is there someone I might appreciate more if I look below their surface?

Up for devo - Emmies TV Book and worked Puzzle - mailed 3 letters to 1st Evan - meet 3rd daughter of family having babies - has 5 yr. old having trouble in Kindergarten. Home to pool. Stretch - racked leaves - Looked at Sports Illustrated photos - - some Bridge & solitaire - Water Emi's flowers - front & back - Clean up grill - Made oven - start fire & cook Chicken - everyone liked dinner - See Peyton & Colts - Ek out Eli & Giants - bad call stops Giant final drive - Eli throws for 2 TD's not as sharp as experienced brother.

And fear not them which kill the body, but are not able to kill the soul. . . . —MATTHEW 10:28

SEPTEMBER 11

WHAT QUALITIES DO I CONSIDER ESSENTIAL TO MY CHARACTER?

Devo - Puzzles - Goff water Forrest - Walter - Chas - 2 balls in street on # 8 retrieve them - scorpion 11" on the hole - see Candy - Home to pool - Kelly cuts grass - Ann to Beatrix + gets Kelly to smell songs - Listen to music and nap - stretched early - lift weights - Walk over for chicken left overs - see old (39) movie Eleanore Powell - Robert __, Geo. + Gracie Allen dual roles -- stupid - Ann correct watch - See Dick Cavett - Characters from Exodus - Burned officer @ Pentagon - (Asian) girl tortured - monster U.S. (Tibet) - Iranian teacher - Holocost survivor in California - Having naps - Woman drugged nursing with 2 babies -

September 12

He who has ears to hear, let him hear.
—Matthew 11:15 (RSV)

IF I SIT SILENTLY FOR A MOMENT DURING THE DAY, WHAT SOUNDS WILL I NOTICE?

Turn down early cold — No Sico + puzzles. Am off to circle meeting — I stretch + walk — see Betty Jop. who rides with Ann to brush + de-leaf pool — Read sports illustrated book -- calls from Bug man + Maine open house.

Drive to Fresh Market for Salmon, milk, cereal. See Gigi -- + eat early. See CSI - Harmon resigns — Ship blows up — See Veronica Mars — violent — Her Dad gets case of money + doesn't see her off.

T.V. schedule messed up — More Murders in Memphis —

No rain — water backyard flowers —

Start plans for nxt Wed. meeting.

I understand more than the ancients,
Because I keep Your precepts.
—Psalm 119:100 (NKJV)

September 13

How can I follow God's laws more closely?

Puzzle — missed punch line — Devo — Off to golf with Walter & Chas — birdie on #7 — Home to cereal — No nap — stretch lift weights — walked with Ann & saw Abbey — Like See John Wayner Horse soldiers — Douglas — sink submarine — & get rich — Read Paul — phoned for prescrip — went buy for sunglasses & Ambien info — blasted & tested pool — watered front flowers — Sunb falls on roof — Called Jack Jackson —

September 14

"Because you are precious in my eyes, and honored, and I love you. . . ."
—Isaiah 43:4 (RSV)

Do I truly believe in God's unconditional love for me?

Ye shall be comforted. . . . —Ezekiel 14:22

September 15

WHAT CAN I DO TO RELAX WHEN I FEEL THAT MY BEST IS NOT GOOD ENOUGH?

SEPTEMBER 16

God setteth the solitary in families. . . .
—Psalm 68:6

What blessings can I find in daily chores around my house?

Thur:

Devo - Russ + 2 Comm R
Am off to 1st Evan -
Golf with Chuck + Walter
par 4 holes 42!
Home to pooh + deodorant + off to
1st Evan with Cam - No nap -
a bit of solitaire + Bridge -
late cereal lunch - Mark over for
chicken + rice dinner -
See few minutes of T.b. Death with
Robert. Jackie Chung movie -
Some Woody Allen + some CSI which
was confusing! Bomb makers in W.
TN. - two murders die - one by hanging
- other cancer -

Sing and make music in your heart to the Lord, always giving thanks to God the Father for everything. . . . —EPHESIANS 5:19–20 (NIV)

SEPTEMBER 17

IN WHAT AREA OF MY LIFE CAN I TAKE THE TIME TO MAKE AN EXTRA EFFORT?

Fri -

Crmme. Puzzle - Devo Finished reading book on Paul - very good writing Went to Skew for Blood commun test — on to Dee's for glass cases take flowers to girls -- Home to nap — + puzzle with Ann. See News - eat veggie supper see Hit battles -- Numbers + more advanced weapons Nazi were working on

MUS loses again - Germ. + CBHS win Olive Br. 56 to 0 over Treadwell

left weights walk with Ann -

September 18

For the Lord is a sun and shield. . . .
—Psalm 84:11 (NAS)

DO I KNOW WHEN TO STAND BACK AND ALLOW OTHERS TO TAKE THE LEAD?

Mon.

2 puzzles - Devo -
Exercise - to Ike's
for drugs -
Home to cereal r
Tooth Brush &
Back wash - Mark & Margie
over for dinner -
See some P.H - Flu game
some CSI -
Go to Kristies game -
canceled --
Read 'old' health book -

> *Be kindly affectioned one to another....*
> —Romans 12:10

SEPTEMBER 19

WHAT LIFE LESSONS HAVE I LEARNED THAT I MIGHT PASS ALONG TO OTHERS?

Devo & puzzler - off to Drs. driving Bubba - Meet beautiful Nashville girl who I kiss goodbye - Gene Fagumi's wife & Hubby in office - Home to cereal - Anne finally gets out of Dr's office & runs errands. I stretch - lift weights & walk during Smile Show - see Bible catastrophic Earthquakes - floods - Jeremy & Bob Fyns came by - I got Dixie for veggie foods - see some of Nova about Einstein's theory. Kidnapped child found safe. Attempt to take 10 yr old Aubrey on path to school - Go to Wild Oats... fix cereal. Kelly cuts lawn - Anne trims & sets out door flowers. Let Kaplan's in phone & Debbie - about party.

SEPTEMBER 20

Strait is the gate, and narrow is the way, which leadeth unto life. .... —Matthew 7:14

LORD, PLEASE HELP ME ON MY PATH THROUGH LIFE.

Devo - Puzzle - Golf with Forrest, Walter, OH + Bavis - we were all lousy - esp. me. Home to blow patio - nap - vack floors - arrange CD's - Help Ann prepare for party.

Big crowd - everyone but Robert's woman. Katelin here with Debbie + Howard - Henry tells - Mindy doesn't stop.

Everyone enjoyed - Ann did great - announced try for another Neighborhood watch.

See Kidnapped - (another 24) last 2.2 weeks.

More violent news plus Germantown abuse.

> "The Lord himself goes before you and will be with you. . . . Do not be afraid. . . ."
> —Deuteronomy 31:8 (NIV)

September 21

What task might I say "yes" to when I am tempted to say "no"?

Leff y out & Golf with Walter & Chas - Walter picup a early - late for us - 44 - 2 doubles -

Ann gets cold but goes to Bible Study - we don't make it to 1st Even - stretch & do weights after nap - Go get prescription for Ann at Skis - Later go get Claritin for Mark & Ann & me - long wait -

See Ga. Tech - win - a much DVD of Mark goes to School - See new series - Defense lawyer goes to prosecute - girl does video of sex & stabs & kills boy -

Admits @ trial - His daughter elects to live with Dad - knife welder starts fire - dies dragged out by cops -

September 22

Blessed are they that do his commandments, that they may have right to the tree of life, and may enter in through the gates into the city.
—Revelation 22:14

Where in nature do I encounter reminders of God's eternal love?

Puzzles - Ann skips
dentist - Read from
Prayer book (1½)
Stretch - walk a lot
work pool - leaves off
TGD - brush - & back wash -
Eat beef stroganov - see - some
W. Weber / We did a game - Neo. wins -
see Law & Order - news -
Get Mail - garbage cans -

Make a joyful noise unto the Lord....
—Psalm 98:4

September 23

DO I ALLOW MYSELF TO PRAISE GOD LOUDLY IN SONG?

7:00 - Am. Puzz. - Walk with Margie - Watch football most all day - See Mich St. over Notre Dame - Ky plays Fla. Gard. - Two roughing penalties cause two TDs - Ohio State over Pa. State - by wins luckily with 2 4th Quarter TDs by sub quarterback. Slip away to buy lottery tickets while Cenn is at Sam's with Kelly - Lifted weights -

SEPTEMBER 24

*As one whom his mother comforteth,
so will I comfort you. . . .* —Isaiah 66:13

LORD, HELP ME FIND WAYS TO SOOTHE THE GRIEF OF A LOVED ONE.

Corn Puzz - Stretch - To 1st Evan Celine. Ann doesn't feel that well - P - Ann Tummy upset. Clean out grill Mask + I cook Pork Chops. Clean pool of leaves - Top + bottom - Kids over for Dinner

SEPTEMBER 25

And a little child shall lead them. —Isaiah 11:6

WHAT CAN I DO TO HELP CHILDREN WHO HAVE LOST THEIR PARENTS?

Cross. Puzzle — off 8
Golf with Chas - Forrest
& Walter after — I stretch
+ lift weights — Poor
shooting. To Ike's for prescriptions
+ to Fresh Market for Roses — cereal
Milk + compliment cashier.
   Work pool for leaves & brush
bottom — Mark + Marie over —
   See N.O. beat Atlanta in
newly done Super Dome --
   see some Dinner at 8 with Barrymores
Oz Angel + Jean Harlow —
   See lot of Cuba's Castro —
Evil dictator —
   News —

SEPTEMBER 26 28

*And you, that were sometime alienated . . .
in your mind . . . yet now hath he reconciled.*
—COLOSSIANS 1:21

WHERE IN MY RELATIONSHIPS IS THERE AN OPPORTUNITY TO MAKE PEACE?

Devo - Puzzles - Ann off to 2nd Pres. Bible study - I read ½ of Guidepost - see end of Pal Joey - Work pool - leaves & brush bottom - see crosswd puzz with Ann - win Bridge Rubber & solitaire - To 1st Dorm for lunch + service - see news for 1-1½ hrs - eat cereal + bread + P.Butter for supper - few bites of Ice cream - see - Boston Pops & N.O. Players - some of Grey's anat. - poor! Ugly Betty - good - Some Auburn S. Carolina Game -

Last nite Dreams - saw 3 loaded trucks - one settles thru log bridge - means won financially - Notre Dame playing while we see something else - Year of Miss. State / TN Game & Fair
Driving with couple - $4 must have been copy of Lottery winner.

Behold, I send an Angel before thee, to keep thee in the way.... —EXODUS 23:20

SEPTEMBER 27

IS THERE A GRIEVING FAMILY WHO NEEDS MY HELP?

Puzzler — Devo — To golf with Burrus + Walter — Ann to Exercise Home — get Kelly on roof + Get limb down — He cuts grass — Then takes him to have car fixed — I talk to him — try to assure him about his situation — Get fish dinner — See Lottery winners + their fate — See CSI New York — 3 girls rob jewels — one killed by African diamond seller — Husband kills wife — Body in abandoned building —

Bush here to find reason to do Iker — Cleo to stop using Venezuelan gas after their Pres. puts down Bush — Mps #2 crime center in U.S.

SEPTEMBER 28 26

"Lo, I am with you always. . . ."
—Matthew 28:20 (RSV)

HOW CAN I HONOR THE MEMORY OF A DEPARTED LOVED ONE?

2 Puzzles + Devo — Golf with Walter + Charlie 43 — lead group — Bill Muller joins us — Home + puter games — naps — work Pool — water Ann's flowers — Read Baseball — Gehrig — Mays — Robinson... Eat Pork chop + salads See House — Read from Prayer Book... See Smith + news — Robbery at quick restaurant — foiled — 3 arrests — Fox Channel 13 — administrator pleads guilty to child rape in Maryland 30 years ago —

Comfort ye, comfort ye my people, saith your God. —ISAIAH 40:1

SEPTEMBER 29

DO I REACH OUT IN KINDNESS TO PEOPLE I DON'T KNOW?

Puzzles – Devo – Work pool – So to Mps Pool for winter treatment – To Sterno for blood test. Trisha – for as Kiss a – Puter Bridge – & Solitaire – Came to Sam's with Kelly whose car was over there – Jim Wilson comes by to check pool pump – almost miss him he was after 12 getting here.
 – Cereal & chicken soup dinner – See Ghost Whisperer & some of Gracey's choice – Veronica Mars with black lover – + Close to Home & Numbers – Murderess Mother seeks daughter & kidnaps female agent –
 Mom killing – Cops vs. Prop. Tax raise – Bush lying about Iraq – Kissinger involved? Repub. congressman resigns – courting teen-age page – after leading against it –

SEPTEMBER 30

O Lord our Lord, how excellent is thy name in all the earth! . . . —PSALM 8:1

WITH THE WONDER OF A CHILD, WHAT SMALL PART OF CREATION CAN I APPRECIATE THIS WEEK?

Vacted ½ pool - Ann & ~~Sams~~ grocery - Ruth over - we walked. Walked football - TN. kills Memphis. LSU over Miss. State. Ky. wins Fla & Ga win. Mich over Mich - Ohio State vs. Iowa - Wash State & S. Cal close -

> *Be ye therefore merciful, as your Father also is merciful.* —LUKE 6:36

OCTOBER 1

HOW DO I SHARE GOD'S GRACE WITH OTHERS?

Vaced 1/2 pool — Did Puzzle — Ann to grocery — to 1st Evan — When is Christ coming — available — here now — James + Peter — Vaced house when C/ appeared — Martha (Adele's helper) visits with 3 yr old daughter — Gives me 5 $ to get her goodies back — Fill water Slover. Mark helps finish — Everyone late to supper except Cel & Ruth —
  Get pool cover on before cooking Steak with Mark — fine dinner — Mikey's B.D. — Ann gives him cash —
  See Without a Trace — Strip club blackmail — mother stripper killed — Hubby no help —

October 2

What time I am afraid, I will trust in thee.
—Psalm 56:3

When was a time that leaning on God strengthened my faith?

Puzzle - Devotional. Off to golf with Forrest, Walter & Burns - Par 4 holes for +3. Water 42. Home to tuna lunch with Quettie — Al. They head for Nashville - See part of Eastwood Keller movie - awful - Do Stretch early. Go to Kristi's Volley Ball - lose in 5 games. See some of Jane Withers - & 3 others little of child stardom - with Mark - some of news show - bad - CSI - bad - some Packer Eagle game - robbery of shapes at Poplar near Overton park - Shoulder didn't hurt at golf.

Blessed are ye that weep now: for ye shall laugh.
—Luke 6:21

OCTOBER 3

LORD, GIVE ME THE ABILITY TO FIND THE HUMOR IN MY MISTAKES.

Devo - Most of USA Puzz. Stretch ½ - lift weights at 6:00 P.M. - Go to David's for check after Pool Service for Skimmer Gizmos. Go get Chicken for supper - see former TV announcer Dave Hucall? who is less than friendly - 6 ft. 6 in. - little wife. See some of Woody Allens - Annie Hall & Law & Order - Killer kills self - see Smith take armored car - wife is catching on. He sees her follow him. Cops catch one drive-way robber. Amish school girls killed-yesterday - on news tonight - Co. school grading system purchase - not working. Mayor goes before board for prop. Tax raise... Fla US Rep. admits he's gay & was molested as young teen by Pastor --

October 4

The end of a matter is better than its beginning, and patience is better than pride.
—Ecclesiastes 7:8 (NIV)

Am I patient with my neighbors and colleagues?

Devo - Puzzle - Stretch some - off to Exercise - Then Ike's for drugs & window spray - Home to cereal & read entire book of Joshuah - victories in which they kill all captives - Divide land between 12 tribes - Minus Levis (priests - who get farm land) Idol - causes trouble but it was a symbol of god. Shat nap - Spray windows front & back of house - water all flowers and wash two cars - see some Raymond -- see CSI NY - young woman kills for bros. revenge - crippled - Boy kill girl friend turned dancer - Arson in town - 3 homes burned 2 criminals caught. House speaker - & gay workers protect gay Fla. rep. who returns -

In his heart a man plans his course, but the Lord determines his steps. —Proverbs 16:9 (NIV)

October 5

WHEN DID I LET GO OF MY EXPECTATIONS, ONLY TO BE PLEASANTLY SURPRISED BY THE RESULTS?

Devo - USA Puzzle (most) off to golf with Chas & Furvest. Home for shower & off to 1st Evan. with Ann to hear about Elijah face the Baal prophets sorta nap - work commercial Puzzle call Furvest about Church golf Tourney - - Call Beak about Evan - Furvest calls back - walk - left weights & stretch - had to leave golf after 8 holes - see news after Raymond - See Ugly Betty & Chubby model - see Mets beat Dodgers behind Glavin - see NC State beat Fla. St. See Shark & Dad kill Mom by accident & little girl testify - see some keeping up - cocktail & house survey - Mark over for bought beef & potato dinner - good -

October 6

Whatever is true, whatever is noble, whatever is right, whatever is pure, whatever is lovely, whatever is admirable—if anything is excellent or praiseworthy—think about such things.
—Philippians 4:8 (NIV)

Do I welcome the opportunity to show hospitality to others?

FRI - Do puzzle. Go see Bubber in afternoon - He seemed fine - Talked clearly - Outline plan for prayer - Drain pump & filter - connect end of vac. hose - Water Ann's flowers & indoor fern. Big fire downtown - Mark checks structure of burned out building from fireman's hoisted tub - Has to go tomorrow - Walk with Ann & Margie. Get treadmill and assemble mostly - it with Ann's diagram help. - See numbers & part of Hitler's family - Whitestater beats Germantown in O.T. CBHS slaughters MHS. Eat left over beef & taters from last night - Marg out of school today - Get call from bank - & Roberta for Ann.

> "I will settle them in their homes," declares the Lord. —Hosea 11:11 (NIV)

OCTOBER 7

DO I TAKE STEPS TO KEEP MY FAITH FRESH?

Devo - Core, Buzz. Stretch & lift weights - See Football games. Fla. over Miss.Take. Prone LSU - TN over Ga. Ark. over Auburn. S. Car. over Ky. by one TD - Detroit knocks Yanks out of play offs - in AL. - Mets beating Dodgers. Put treadmill back together with Ann's help - She gets dizzy. Roberta calls for Ann - Mary comes over - Early with cookies - I don't leave house. Check out prayer outline - Ann to grocery - sees Bubber who is better -
Adelle on last days —

OCTOBER 8

He who tends a fig tree will eat its fruit. . . .
—Proverbs 27:18 (NIV)

WHAT SMALL ACTS OF KINDNESS CAN I PERFORM TODAY?

Comm. Puzzle - Start little vac - after dinner. off & 1st Evan - Then to Sam's with Ann & get cooked chicken - candy & video game.
Little & big vac entire house - Watch football - see Eagles win -
Family over for supper - watch games - San Diego beats Pittsburg -
Cardinals win over Padres 3 games to one - Play Mets Wed. & work toward 7 game W. Series start.
Detroit has beat Yanks 3 g. to 1
Another fire Mud Island complex - Bad sauna wiring starts it.
Termites made rotten embers fly from 1st Church to 3 other bldgs.
House in S. Memphis burns - See. Without a Trace - Raped girl nearly kills wrong Dr.
Talk to Ernest Hughes - & Burris & off tomorrow

> "'For I know the plans that I have for you,' declares the Lord. . . ." —Jeremiah 29:11 (NAS)

OCTOBER 9

WHEN DID GOD'S PLANS EXCEED MY EXPECTATIONS?

Devo – Puzzle – Stretch – off to golf with Walter – Forrest, Chas & Jim – walked 9 – Home to lite lunch – partial nap – blew leaves off pool cover & patio – watered all back yard plants. Petted neighbor cat – wch bridge – Mary Jo calls – Boodie giving up her home & we decide to spend Neb in Harrodsburg – 14½ – to Center & Fri. 19th – lift weights – Musk over & Eat left-overs see Laurel & Hardy script – See Egypt Engineers – See CSI Miami – 4 Murders – No Arson in Church fire – Naked Man in convenience store – Ann Miller Mon. aft. Meet – Take bath & do my Nails – Read some of Sun. bulletin –

October 10

Lead me in thy truth, and teach me. . . .
—Psalm 25:5

Does my faith in God give me confidence to share it with others?

Devo - Puzzles - Ann off to CWF with Devotional - Golf with Jervesi, Walter & Burris - Walter will play in Tourney with us - no Jim - To Wild Cats - Alice's (no lunch) & to AARP for motel reservation in Harrodsburg - Partial nap & off to Kristie's volleyball game — they lose 3 straight - To Schimuli's for dinner - see Detroit over Oakland 6-1 in 9th. -
CSI - we killer experimentor - from Germany - see Much of Hush - Saved Charlotte - she kills Calista & Haerland & Wells Co-Star — Betty was innocent but she thought otherwise - off to mrs house more shootings in mps - Treadwell Hi car Jack —
I think cancelled —
Hist - see Tsunami (over 200,000 deaths) & Yellowstone threat -

Jerusalem remembers in the days of her affliction . . . all the precious things that were hers from days of old. . . .
—LAMENTATIONS 1:7 (RSV)

OCTOBER 11

WHAT IS MY FAVORITE MEMORY OF MY CHILDHOOD?

Devo - USA Puzzle - off to Exercise - then Ike's cereal after nap in living Room - Ann off to group friend delivery - Let Ruth in and get lunch for her - Ann back & takes Ruth to Memorial funeral Home - Read Guidepost - win rubber & some solitaire - see News - & eat dinner & fruit salad - see Detroit beat A's & lead 2-0 - Cards-Mets rained out - see M.O. Jazz band & news - called Lindenwood golf arranger - a walter for Friday match - cuil get Burris or Forrest Kelly & Britt cut grass - Ann gives Britt $20 extra which I keep snatching - Pet Cat.

October 12

> Jesus often withdrew to lonely places and prayed.
> —Luke 5:16 (NIV)

How can I refresh my faith with a moment of solitude?

Devo - Puzzle - Ann off to 2nd Pres - A walk - left weights later - Iso & 1st evan. + don't eat Home to Ann - she goes to store for items. I study prayer book - Talk to ~~David~~ Forrest. Burris & Walter - about golf arrangements Call Boodie about Fri nite Trip w Harrodsburg - Ask her not to cook Saturday - Go from Church to get flu test - Flirt w/the girls & patients - lite rain --- Music over for Bar-b-Q + ugly Betty - who gets neighborhood expert photog to do issue - Vanessa breaks everything in home - mystery ~~woman calls~~ about new Easter's Dad + car lot. Nats beat Cards 3-0 Glavin winner - 2 run homer Marx Bros. @ races -- Sharks wins court case by finding weapon - actor guilty

Cease from anger, and forsake wrath. . . .
—Psalm 37:8

OCTOBER 13

DO I RECOGNIZE OPPORTUNITIES TO REPLACE ANGER WITH KINDNESS?

Devo - Stretch - off to Lindenwood Tourney + Shoot par with Walter - Forrest + Chas. - One Birdie - one Bogie - Play Ed G - Got gas on Summer + home to see Wendy + pal come in and leave - Then return - See Numbers Ghost toriflu - since of Card / Mets game - Cards lead by 3 in top of 9th Close to home also - Serial Killer Father - named by daughter - Family of 4 murdered off highway in Fla. - See Brian + wife Rose + Mike - Bill Harris - Jim Cunalli - Bob + son + grandson - Nutt - Chasity + Mimi - - - -

October 14

There are varieties of working, but it is the same God who inspires them all in every one.
—I Corinthians 12:6 (RSV)

GOD, HELP ME TO APPRECIATE DIFFERENT PATHS TO THE SAME GOAL.

Devo - Conc. Puzzle - To Adele's funeral with Ann + Margie - Mark there - has to leave for Cell University game. which they lost on last Hail Mary Pass. Home from funeral to cereal - Then to Burial ceremony at Memorial Building Casket bldg. - attacked by Gnats - Home to ball games. Alabama beats Ole Miss at end of game - Auburn upsets Fla - Michigan over Penn State. Ky drubbed by LSU - Ga. beaten at home by underdog Vandy - Detroit beats Oakland + in World Series - St Louis over Mets - Wendy + Rita here for Bar B Q. Hey Lenny - then take Ruth home -
See Ann Bancroft in Miracle Worker -

He gives food to every living thing, for his lovingkindness continues forever.
—Psalm 136:25 (TLB)

OCTOBER 15

DO I TAKE MULTIPLE OPPORTUNITIES TO THANK GOD FOR BLESSINGS?

Devo Work Puzzle Wendy & Rita run for her. To 1st Even. - Tell Blunt's date to chain her to his belt. Home to Prayer - see some football Ready B-B-Q. -- with Mark - Britt's B.D. - Ann gives away her money + present - Kids really after each other -- See Without a Trace crippled boy puts sister in basement - more crier in Mps. -

October 16

Love never fails. . . . —I Corinthians 13:8 (NIV)

Does love guide my interactions each day?

Devo - 2 puzzles. To exercise after lifting weights - Rain most of gloomy day. Take 6 entree - to Karen @ David's office. Ann to small group. Mark + Marge over - see some of Millsburg comeback in football. See HoCen - game rained out in St Louis.

He rested on the seventh day from all his work which he had made. —GENESIS 2:2

OCTOBER 17

HOW CAN I INCORPORATE A TIME OF REST AND REJUVENATION INTO MY DAILY SCHEDULE?

Vero - csu. Buzz — to haircut & Joe McCampbell — to bank & Wild Oats. To Mercedes & wes fixes too fried-weather holes up to sharp tooth -- learn that he is training for Marathon - To Bubba's with Oat cereal which Ruth gets. Leave early with USA paper & do puzzle -- Pump pool - see water - see News - - eat hamburger dinner. See Cardenals beat Mets 4-2 -

Some News - 2 plane crash (747) on runway in Caribbean - ? See Betty Hutton life on T.V. — treated badly by crew on set of Annie Get your Gun by Howard Keel & Ed Wynn Jr.. See Annie Get your Gun too

October 18

For if they fall, the one will lift up his fellow. . . .
—Ecclesiastes 4:10

Which of my friends needs extra support from me this week?

Wed - Britt's 15th B.D. Devo + Puzzle (almost). Go to AAA & Ike's + Jeremy's Phys. Therapy. See Deb. + Flower girl. Go to Cuccles' visitation & David's Morgan Keegan party at Brod's Rest — eat plenty. Home to see Cards lose + part of Samson & NY Crime. Kelly cuts grass & tapes side mirror — get gas for car — Pumps pool cover a lot. Ann plants flowers & gets her hair done. Mark & Mary over to say goodbye

Let us take our journey, and let us go. . . .
—Genesis 33:12

October 19

AM I UNDERTAKING A JOURNEY ON WHICH I NEED GOD'S HELP?

Call Debbie & Hallie about our leaving town. Head for Cave City, Ky. Eat at Cracker Barrel for supper - Drive through constant rain & terrible traffic -
Stay at Super 8 -

October 20

Give instruction to a wise man, and he will be yet wiser: teach a just man, and he will increase in learning. —Proverbs 9:9

How has my knowledge influenced someone else?

Drive to Harrodsburg Beaumont Inn - check it out before checking in at Day's Inn - under wrong AAA Name - good thing we had street address - sit by Ed Bell & Bess & Mary + Bob for lunch. Look over Campus @ Centre + go to Contributor's dinner at Gymnasium. See Susie + President - & eat with Tom + Barbie. See Bushes + McMasters. - Bob Hill going down hill with diabetes +. See Milan & Tom Stewart - Rosenberg - Betty M. & Jean Van Grunigon - To Days Inn for end of close & Home - ending at 10 Eastern Time.

> Blessed is the man whose strength is in You,
> whose heart is set on pilgrimage.
> —Psalm 84:5 (NKJV)

October 21

LORD, WHEN I WALK THROUGH A VALLEY, HELP ME TO KEEP MY FOCUS ON YOU.

Saturday. Get to President's house reception - get retired lady-faculty member's picture with President - kid Susie - No Ralls there - Hear about alumni affairs + affairs - tell to a number of tables.

To football game - sit with Tam & Barbie + Burva - leave at half with Centre down 14-0 -

See past of Rhodes Centre girl's Volley Ball contest - Rhodes winning 1st 30 pt. match -

To Rosemary's for fancy prime rib dinner - Ruth's there with Bob & Mary - Meet Ed's old golf mate.

Drive to Lex - can't find gas station or Boodie's at. Eaton Bars Ga. Fla. address - Watch Ga. Tech. die before Clemson & St. Louis down Detroit in World S.

October 22

The Lord God has given Me the tongue of disciples, That I may know how to sustain the weary one with a word.... —Isaiah 50:4 (NAS)

When did I last share an inspirational story with someone?

Fill in this date book - Ann has mild headache which gets us out of trip to Natural Bridge - cereal with Choc. Blueberries. Bath - see sisters off to N. Bridge - We head for Nashville - Get there before Cal & Ruth - Cal & I go get Chinese and Milk - See Balt. win - To bed after huge dump.

To be spiritually minded is life and peace.
—Romans 8:6

OCTOBER 23

DO I RECOGNIZE EVERYDAY BLESSINGS ALONG WITH EVERYDAY MISHAPS?

Up to Eye Dr. — We load up and take off for Memphis — Easy ride — clear skies. Call Boodie & learn that Wm. Everet's heart murmurs take entire 15 kinfolks to Hospital — Chas. & Boodie go to Hazelgreen & listen to Steve — talk all the ceremony. Boodie with boys & Daniel thanks due for mercy. Call Bessie — no ans. Call Becky no ans. Call Boodie to learn they are all at her house — Talk to Macey + 3 kids — Steph & Kate thank me. Bay doesn't but learns to play dominos — Mark over for my 8 piece chicken dinner — Thanks over — See Grants beating Dallas —

October 24

Blessed are the peacemakers: for they shall be called the children of God. —Matthew 5:9

Do I help to achieve peace in my community?

Leave ~~for Memphis~~ — ~~Easy trip~~ — Stretch — Golf with Chas & Wallis & Torrey — We play badly. Birdie 4 with off green putt — —

Home to cereal — Read Sports Illustrated — listen to music but can't nap — Veggie supper and see Detroit lose to St Louis with lousy fielding & uncontrolled pitching — Took Hot tub before golf —

The Lord my God will enlighten my darkness.
—Psalm 18:28

October 25

WHAT CAN I DO TO BE MORE CHEERFUL DURING THE STORMS OF MY LIFE?

Worked cm. puzzle + started USA - geg to exercise + to Ike's for drugs - rains all day drizzle -- Go in store for purse - coughing cashier - other one caught it as I was leaving - Wash 2 cars - Ann to Bubba's with veggies - I eat ham sandwich too fast - get nap after depressed day - coffee + latte own trip with Ann - stretch + left weights - see news - eat burger over veggies and fruit salad for supper - World Series game rained out - see Sandra Bullock + English Hugh Grant in movie - He saves her Coney Island play house + loses job - Manatee still swimming in Wolf River port --- Political T.V. attack ads time -

October 26

Let the beauty of the Lord our God be upon us. . . . —Psalm 90:17 (NKJV)

Whose inner beauty impresses me? Why?

Devo + 2 Puzzles
Ann off to 2nd Pres - Bible study - Bubba calls about his paper put in car port - Walk in house & do stretches. Go to 1st Evan with Ann to lunch service - drizzle rain most of day - Read weight loss book.
    See news - Manatee disappears from Wolf River - Mark & Marg. over for Spaghetti. See Ungy Betty - World Series & Shark - Tiger pitchers have made 4 errors - a series record.
    Tigers tie game in 8th
    I get nap & so does Ann...
    "Fake" cop robs 2 Truck drivers & lady in Motel - badge works -
    Marshmellow gets me on USA puzzle Harold Ford tape phone call + Lamar Alexander too - Playboy girl ad not done by Rep. Committee - but TV guy in Dallas
    Lies about source

When I consider thy heavens, the work of thy fingers, the moon and the stars, which thou hast ordained; What is man, that thou art mindful of him? . . . —PSALM 8:3–4

OCTOBER 27

WHAT OPPORTUNITY CAN I TAKE TO ADMIRE THE HEAVENS?

Devo — 2 puzzles — Stretch & Lift weights — Go to Sterni's for blood test — blood too thick — Nap — read from Spts. Illustrated walk & jog 10 minutes — Pump pool cover — Watch news — one Raymond Eat Bubba's chicken & fruit salad see Cardinals win W.S. final 4–2 — Detroit error's threw game away — hitting pitiful — Former Detroit pitcher wins game for Cards See Numbers — some Great Pumpkin — some History —

October 28

Encourage the timid, help the weak, be patient with everyone. —I Thessalonians 5:14

How am I blessed when I give my time to help others?

Deco - Clim, Puzz - Drained pool cover & got leaves to corners - Ky beats Miss State. TN edges out S. Carolina - Fla. von Georgia - Oregon State upsets USC - Memphis loses big to Marshall - Ken & Betty drive to see it. Britt goes with Conner to Minn. St. game - Betty Lyons in Hosp - Aunt Sarah's sister Kelly - Then to grocery - I stretch & wade off/an in horse - - Ga. Tech wins over Miami - Eat spaghetti supper -

Then Job reported to the Lord: "I know that you can do all things; no plan of yours can be thwarted." —Job 42:1–2 (NIV)

OCTOBER 29

WHAT FRUSTRATIONS IN MY PAST HAVE BEEN PROVIDENTIAL?

Puzzle - To 5th Evan - Over to see Betty Lyons at Baptist - Work on pool cover - Trimming and leafing - See Colts win over Denver @ Denver - . Kids over for Roast supper - left weights and stretch - work on siner problems twice - Dallas beat Carolina - Rutgers over Connecticut - See End of exorcist -- and some without a trace - Murdered man has dogs that need adoption -- Read complete mag. - Guideposts Vuch floors —

OCTOBER 30

> *Be strong and of a good courage....*
> —DEUTERONOMY 31:6

WHEN HAVE I BEEN CALLED TO SUMMON MY COURAGE?

PUSH Puzz. Devo — Pump pool cover — Golf with Charlie & Walter — Par #3 and a sandy par on 9 — Wall & pull cart — Home to blow leaves & pump & use pool brush — Quite a workout. Won Bridge Rubber — See news — Read from battles of Civil War — Check & use prayer devotion book — We watch Shane on tape — See some of Armenian genocide and New Eng. leading Minn — Rain predicted for tomorrow —

Be on the alert. Your adversary . . . prowls about . . . seeking someone to devour.
—I Peter 5:8 (NAS)

OCTOBER 31

What fears do I need to take to God in prayer?

Devo - & 2 Puzzles - Anne off to Bcl meet @ Fendenwood + Circle at Nell's - + lunch - I go to Wild Oats & Fresh Market scared by Halloween salmon seller -
  Home to Battles of Civil War + devotion prayer book - & glimpse of Diet book - walk in pool over some - lift weights and take Hot Tub for sore Back -
  Eat fish + potatoes for supper - See some of Nova's Black hole and History - House - & E on Hollywood murders - Simpson - Manson - Blake - Murder suicides
  See CSI New York + some of U. Price + House of Usher -
  News - Kerry talks about dumb people going to Iraq -
  Getting colder -

NOVEMBER 1

The people that walked in darkness have seen a great light.... —ISAIAH 9:2

DO I SEE AN OPPORTUNITY TO BE A SOURCE OF LIGHT IN SOMEONE ELSE'S LIFE?

2 Puzzles - Devo - Call Karen @ David's office - $500 - Drive to Exercise + To Kroger for Milk + orange punch. Bug Man there - go to vote early + joke with crowd - To Baptist - see Betty Lyons - Chalyn and Nadine Ditzel. Home to nap - cold dreary day - see News - some Raymond. Eat Salmon + Potato leftovers with fruit salad. Check prayer devotional - see Va. Tech over Clemson - Mystery of serial killer + "Friends" star in murder + kidnap mystery - Grizzlies - lose to Nicks here by one point - Miller misses last shot -

"As for me, I would seek God . . . who does great things and unsearchable, marvelous things without number." —JOB 5:8–9 (RSV)

NOVEMBER 2

DO I USE ALL OF MY GOD-GIVEN SENSES TO EXPERIENCE THE WORLD?

Devo - Puzzle - Stretch - off to Cendalon with Walter & Ches. - Par 5 holes for 42 - two doubles (42-) Home to pack cooler & Map - lunch at 4:00 pm.

Mash over - Leave Kelly's soup & Bar-b-que sauce - fruit salad - see ugly Betty - cheif problems with Dad who tells boss & runs away with his wife -- Vanessa has trouble with her daughter -

See Louisville beat Virginia Tech see some of the Chiefs - Shark - News & Camp.

NOVEMBER 3

"Surely God is my salvation; I will trust and not be afraid. . . ." —Isaiah 12:2 (NIV)

Are there times in my life when I allow my fears to trap me?

Devo + Puzzle - Golf @ 10 with Forrest - Chas. & Walter - Pier # 8 + 9 - Tie water - Beat others. Home to bath - lunch - dress for visit to Dr. Berry - Then to David's for check - Home for Ann's endorsement & to bank - Home - Do cross. puzzle - Lift weights - see news - Eat Fruit salad - Turnip greens & Ravioli. See ½ of It is on Near to Home & see Air Force beating Army. See Numbers. See MacArthur take Phillipine & free 7,000 prisoners -- See Numbers & some Jet dog-fights on History -

More news of gay preacher - NHS stomped again - Relate station reruns.

> "All my words that I shall speak to you receive in your heart, and hear with your ears."
> —Ezekiel 3:10 (RSV)

NOVEMBER 4

DO I LISTEN CLOSELY TO THE PROMISES OF GOD?

Devo — Puzzle —
Pimp Pool cover —
use blower on leaves
Watch football — LSU over
TN — Ark. over S. Carolina — Oklahoma
over TX. Aggies — Ky. beats Ga.
+ Miss State beats Alabama —
Stretch — walk easy with Meg &
Ann — eat Bacon & eggs supper —
Margie brings Cookies —
Rose by to tell us Susie loses
lawn tools to someone who parked
car in her driveway —
Grizzlies lose to Detroit.
1-2 record.

NOVEMBER 5

"The Lord has kept the promise he made. . . ."
—I Kings 8:20 (NIV)

HOW CAN MY UNSPOKEN LANGUAGE COMMUNICATE GOD'S LOVE?

Devo - Worked puzzle missing 2 letters - To 1st Eden. after bath & shave - Home to rock house & work on pool cover - dragging leaves across - & blowing deck. Fix grill for work on chicken. Mark comes to bring coal's starter - cook chicken with Mark & leave dinner - MSt loses to Southern Miss on ESPN.

Colts upset New England - Manning great. vs. Brady - see delayed 48 hours - girl a suicide -

More murders in Memphis - Halls fire contained - big job - hauling water -

Be careful to maintain good works. . . .
—Titus 3:8

NOVEMBER 6

IN WHAT WAYS CAN I EXPRESS MY GRATITUDE TO THE PEOPLE WHO SUPPORT ME?

Devo USA Puzzle — off to exercise — Home to cereal — Rains nearly all day — Lift weights & stretch — Go to Post Office for special mail — But a mistake —

Mark & Mary over — eat dark chicken & see Above Suspicion — Former Mafia son innocent — daughter finds record book with cops & attorneys involved — partner killed — See some of 2 3/4 hr. 1776 — musical — was on Broadway — See CSI Miami — decapitation by girlfriend — Stolen car racket — More election news — Myts death @ 130 — Call Boochi — can't get Baud shower

NOVEMBER 7

In the fourth year was the foundation of the house of the Lord laid.... —I KINGS 6:37

ON WHAT FOUNDATION DO I BASE MY POLITICAL DECISIONS?

News & Puzzles - walk in house -- Take Ann to Movie - H.S. Football & Religion - liked it - mentioned Jesus - To Wild Oats - for cereal + seed - after Taking Ann to Kroger - pick her up. See lady with huge quantity of paper towels - Pump? pool cover - - ugly day - See Ga. Tech over N.C. in univ. See some house & lot of Rogers & Hammerstein Cinderella - with black Cindy & Oriental prince - who has white father & whooped Goldbrig as mom - Election results. looks as though House goes Republican - Senate still up for grabs. Brandie calls about 'Core Watch' meeting.

Preach the word! Be ready in season and out of season. Convince, rebuke, exhort, with all longsuffering and teaching. —II TIMOTHY 4:2 (NKJV)

NOVEMBER 8

HOW CAN I STRENGTHEN MY FAITH TO MAKE IT EASIER TO SHARE WITH OTHERS?

Devo - USA Puzzle
Stretch - off to golf
certh forest - Chas. & Walter
Played # 8 only -
Walter one under after 3 holes
Home to pump pool cover - Ann to
Exercise & Marie's luncheon - Ann gets
48¢ worth of gas. before getting help -
- Wii viebler & solitaire -
eat chicken soup dinner - lift weights -
see some of Cedars family (weird)
and History on Drugs (2 his) & Tobacco
- See news - Dems have House
& Senate - cerber line rep. winner
Great! —
Rumsfeld fired as director
of Iraq War —

NOVEMBER 9

> They helped every one his neighbour; and every one said to his brother, Be of good courage.
> —Isaiah 41:6

AM I CAREFUL TO CONSIDER SITUATIONS FROM ALTERNATE PERSPECTIVES?

Devo - USA Puzzle - Stretch - Golf with Walter - Donnie - Chas & Me - Jim plays with his Dad - Par 9 + 9 - Home to work on pool cover - Came to Sid Bros + lunch. then to Steve - Read Bible 1 & 2 Peter - Mark over for Fish dinner See - Ugly Betty - + Louisville & Rutgers - tied - See Shark - Collierville schools lockdown Kid with gun -

"The Spirit of the Lord is upon Me. . . . He has sent Me to proclaim release to the captives . . . to set free those who are downtrodden. . . ."
—LUKE 4:18 (NAS)

NOVEMBER 10

IS THERE SOMEONE WHO IS WAITING FOR ME TO GIVE THEM A SECOND CHANCE?

Dodo & Puzzler – Golf with Walter after waiting over 30 minutes for Charlie – who doesn't show – Walter 39 – Me 42 Home to blow leaves in front. – win Bridge & solitaire (twice) See news – one Raymond – See some Wizard of Oz & Barabas with Anthony Quinn – Arthur Kennedy as Caesar – Ernest Borgnine – ½ of Numbers & news – Motorcycle race death – Woman found in pond at Condo area – One string victim heads for 5 yrs jail – Blow back deck too –

November 11

*The Lord will give strength unto his people;
the Lord will bless his people with peace.*
—Psalm 29:11

LORD, HELP ME TO REMEMBER THOSE I KNOW WHO ARE RISKING THEIR LIVES FOR PEACE.

Devo - commercial puzzle. Blow leaves from street & sidewalk & back door walk with troublesome blower. Then mulch all front leaves with mower - quite a sweat! Watch Ga. cream Auburn @ Auburn. See S. Carolina lose by 1 point at Florida - See Arkansas beat Tenn. badly. See LSU beat Alabama - Ky beats Vandy - Oklahoma barely beat Texas Tech. See Memphis lose by 2 points. Watch Texas struggle w/ K. Kansas State. Texas Q.B. out after scoring ouch on first possession - Ann to Sam's and grocery. Bet bacon & egg supper. Tx. closes within 3 with 1 1/2 min. left.

> "Bring the full tithes into the storehouse . . . and thereby put me to the test, says the Lord of hosts. . . ." —MALACHI 3:10 (RSV)

NOVEMBER 12

IN WHAT WAYS CAN I INCREASE MY GIVING?

Slept & less week Ty Pike — Worked puzzle — No kit Even — Home to Blew ground-up leaves in a pile & finished Vacting — Anne goes to Hough's with Keith + Carlotine — buy ornaments — Get cooker ready — See some football — read 1 + 2nd Peter Read John 1, 2, 3 — from Message — She shin B.O. Mark & cook steak in dark. Everyone here for supper — see Westlord & Trace — Delicious textured — NY loses b Bears Colts win again. Bears runs 108 yards after fielding short feet & good — all-time record. Former Titan QB comes to Nashville + beats old team — Great comeback

NOVEMBER 13

"Cease striving and know that I am God. . . ."
—Psalm 46:10 (NAS)

GOD, HELP ME FIND WAYS TO KEEP MY FOCUS ON YOU.

Devo + Puzzle (USA) Wait for Ruth + off to exercise - Lunch + over to Barber's - Go to Dentist - Back to find Al + Ruth loading car - Empty Annie - Ice Cream + Small snack - News - + Steak leftovers with Mark. Margie over too - See videos + Jesse James story - Killed for Reds in Missouri - Frank gets off. Gov. pays Ford to kill Jesse.

See Little Annie Oakley History with Buffalo Bill - Falsely accused by newspapers. Gets 27,000 from Herst - can't find anything wrong with Annie's past - a lady + typical phenom. - Performs in Europe - London + Paris - car/train wreck - car wreck ends career.

In his hand is the life of every creature and the breath of all mankind. —Job 12:10 (NIV)

NOVEMBER 14

HOW CAN I HELP TO MEET THE NEEDS OF GOD'S CREATURES?

Devo — + USA Puzzle — Rest — Cal off weather — Cabelas' can drive thru rain to the river. Came to circle + CWF luncheon — I stretch, lift weight + walk in house 30 minutes — also have phone paces check from Stern's map in A.M. — See Robert Mitchum movie where girl's son kills 4 men, including Mitchum — see son Raymond — eat salmon I got today @ Fresh Market after going to Aker — Give candy — front + back — Rains most of day — also went to Wild Oates. —

See new show @ WBS. some of CSI N.Y. with Harmon. — Channel 10 @ 8:00 — Exposure of Oregon Gay Mayor —

November 15

So the last shall be first, and the first last. . . .
—Matthew 20:16

When was a time that I found myself in a place of humility?

Devo - Puzzles - To exercise with Ann - Go to Ricki's for Kosher desserts - Ann & I got up front leaves & bags - Two trips out for me - small nap. Only ½ banana & P. Butter for Breakfast & cereal for lunch - some Bridge - call from Chas. Burris and Jack Blake - Ann talks to Betty J. - Ann cleans for Tomorrow's party. - See News & Raymond with Robert's I. Q. test - See British bomb development for wrecking German Dams - 6 crews lost 2 dams ruined - 1000 Germans drown - See some of hapless Grizzlies & Vandy See CSI N.Y. - mother kills own daughter.

Thou didst cleave the earth with rivers.
—Habakkuk 3:9

November 16

Do I have a tendency to choose which of God's laws to obey?

Devo. Puzzle — USA — Call from Ann with stalled car. Go take her to Church — call AAA and watch car being loaded — Autorama lets it sit — Service secretary has to go find it after I call AAA.

Go to 1st Ever and meet 3 nice women — esp. one and man who was in class with 18 hot girls in H.S. — Home to nap — Vack Geese + rake leaves on sidewalk —

Lift weights — go get chicken for Mark + me — Ann still full of lunch... Have neighborhood watch meet. Lots of good info —

Lots of talk from Segals + Mandy... Thought they would never leave — see Shark.

2 deputies shot in Fayette Co before shooter is killed —

November 17

Therefore, brethren, stand fast, and hold the traditions which ye have been taught....
—II Thessalonians 2:15

What traditions in my family do I hold dear?

Devo - Puzzle - Call Mercedes on - and in - Wes. Go rest there to thank service girl - she's not in - Give candy - leave. Wes calls later. Go get gas and 5 lottery tickets - Home to read fun book + win bridge rubber. Take Neighborhood watch info to Kaplans + Sharers. Henry + Roberts not in - call both of them.

Give candy to garbage men - They appreciate it - Go in Kaplans + talk to Joan. She's not in good shape.

See Ghost Whisperer - Close to Home - and Monk + part of Numbers.

White Station wins - but Grizzlies lose.

Truth lasts. . . . —Proverbs 12:19 (MSG)

November 18

Have I discovered my own personal truths in my family relationships?

Com. Puzzle & D400 - Watched games — Ole Miss loses to LSU in Overtime - Ark over MS St 28-14 - Ky beats a Mother Team 42-46 - USC over Cal. — Ohio State over Mich. by 3 pts -- TN beats Vandy - Auburn over ALA - close - Rutgers upset by Cincinnati - Go to Barber's with Ann Sarice - his phone sounded busy - had it on - Get Bacon & Egg Supper - blow backyard leaves - for mulching tomorrow - Sleep, prayers back — & outline

NOVEMBER 19

Great peace have those who love Your law. . . .
—Psalm 119:165 (NKJV)

DO I VIEW THE BIBLE AS AN INSTRUCTION MANUAL FOR MY LIFE?

Devo – Puzzle – unfinished – Hot Tub – 1st Even. – Margie there – see Ballengers & their grandson – give candy to out-of-town guests – see Widower – Have to cereal – Tum to grocery – see some TV – & Prayer – 14ds over for Portenders – – See Cath & Manny lose to Dallas – Denver loses at home – see Without a trace & piece of Palm Beach story – news late – stretch & walk 12 minutes

Give thanks to him and praise his name.
—Psalm 100:4 (NIV)

NOVEMBER 20

HOW CAN I BALANCE MY PRAYER REQUESTS WITH EXPRESSIONS OF GRATITUDE?

Devo - Cross. puzzle - up late — Go to golf but too cold to play — go get glasses straight after stepping on them — lifting weights — Did stretch — Ann to circle -- see Ken & Merle over for left-overs - see Charlie Brown + Snoopy teach him to play marbles — see Alabama beat Xavier - Ky. beat De Paul by 7 - Morris + Crawford + Perry - Frosh looked good - Ky. defense not good enough -

NOVEMBER 21

*Because he is at my right hand,
I will not be shaken.* —Psalm 16:8 (NIV)

When was a time that I felt God's reassuring presence with me?

Devo + USA Puzzler Golf w/ Forrest - Walter + Charlie - we all play poorly - Forrest does better. To Wild Oats + Creme of cereal - some puter games - Blow leaves + get Mower going + Grind 'em up. Took about 2 hours.

Eat salmon + carrent soufflé's - See GA. Tech come back from big deficit to beat Memphis.

UCLA leads the early + by big cornt. They get ball inside + get the rebounds. By having to score from outside - Freshmen look good. Lucale Crawford helps on boards + urk Gets 3's - UCLA looks better - getting Ballon follow ups. Can't score ly in paint closer. Going by 20 pts - See some of President on TV - Jackson dictator. Van Buren hurt by economy - Tyler extends US to west + Takes Texas - did well Harrison goes + in mackerel + gets Pneumonia - served 32 days

My flesh and my heart may fail, but God is the strength of my heart and my portion forever.
—Psalm 73:26 (NIV)

November 22

WHEN IN THE PAST HAVE I TURNED MY WEAKNESS OVER TO GOD?

USA pur9 - dues - stretch. Off to Golf with Walter - Chuck-Terrel. Shoot 40 - winner! Walter 41 - Hs 1, 2, 4, 7, 8 - Bogie rest. Me to Alice's. Helen calls me Turkey - Home to rest. See Ky. Lose bad to Mississippi. UCLA leading Ga. Tech big in 2nd half. Myrl + Mary over - Eat pork - Spaghetti - Fruit + bread for supper.

Bruce comes by + gets Mickey from Ann - See Bullock recovery from alcoholic (28 days) movie - see some of Bible Hist. - some of CSI N.Y. + some Medium - some of Garfield movie - Butler beats U.T.

November 23

It is a good thing to give thanks unto the Lord. . . .
—Psalm 92:1

WHEN CAN I TAKE THE OPPORTUNITY TO SHARE MY GRATITUDE TO GOD WITH OTHERS?

Thanksgiving. Devo & Com. Puzzle - Work leaves off pool & pump cover — Mark over - has nap - See Dallas win -
Big dinner @ 2:30 - Great food Sue, Mary & Nancy bring food - Kelly does oysters & cuts Turkey -
Some Solitare - Kids bring up and set Xmas Tree - all delighted - all kinds of desert - pecan pie Key Lime - Choc. cake - Kids enjoy each other - see Ugly Betty - Bud & Jeremy play video games -
See some of White Xmas - Bing & Danny Kaye - Vera Ellen & Rosemary Clooney.
See Shark deal with prostitutes and pimps.
Little girl kidnapped by estranged Father - Mom & sent in Christ.
Too much wind for parade things

Esau ran to meet Jacob and embraced him.... And they wept. —GENESIS 33:4 (NIV)

NOVEMBER 24

WHEN DID I CALL ON GOD-GIVEN WISDOM TO SETTLE A DISPUTE?

Devo - USA puzzle + Commercial Appeal also - See LSU beat Ark. in Little Rock - Okla beats Colorado - Get leaves off pool - wire up front porch Xmas tree. Blow leaves tw. guild up tomorrow - White Station loses State Championship by one touchdown - Olive Branch loses big in front of standing room only crowd - Mark over for supper + 2 drinks - Marg. helps mom with tree decorations - I help a little with reaching boxes on high shelves & taking some to basement - See end of Weeds and Numbers Woman ## teacher murdered in Cordova - Early bath - Ann shops -

NOVEMBER 25

Then God saw everything that He had made, and indeed it was very good. . . . —GENESIS 1:31 (NKJV)

AM I GRATEFUL FOR THE OPPORTUNITY TO WORK HARD?

Devo + Nuzn. Blow leaves - Big day yesterday for leaf fall - Blow Mulch in piles around yard + periodically get leaves off pool - Marcie over - See TN. beat Ky Rsrch 17-12 - We could have won it - delay penalty on 3 yd line - future looks good Okla - over Oklo. State - Wake Forrest wins 1/2 Championship - Plays Ga. Tech next - USC over Notre Dame - a big at end - by N.D. made comeback Geo. beats Ga. Tech - get bacon - egg supper - @ 5:30 - Xmas trees lit up -

It is the Lord your God you must follow, and him you must revere. Keep his commands and obey him; serve him and hold fast to him.
—Deuteronomy 13:4 (NIV)

NOVEMBER 26

LORD, HELP ME TO BE RECEPTIVE TO YOUR GUIDANCE.

Devo + Puzzle –

Up at 8 – Lift weights + stretch watching Colts win. TN. Titans come back from 21-0 to beat N.Y. Eli throws int. giving time for a Titan F.G. with seconds left –

To First Evan. with burping baby in front – Tell ladies about it – they laugh – so does Mom + Dad –

Sermon on Strays. See Believers – Watch 3 Monks on Marathon – One where he gets his reader aid – saves fish instead of moon rock –

– Kids over for leftovers Bruth's B.B. game Wednesday –

See Xmas candles – Mom dies + friends get child –

See some Warren Buffett – in Omaha –

First TN – Waltz felon goes to jail – no map –

NOVEMBER 27

"If you have faith as small as a mustard seed. . . . Nothing will be impossible for you."
—Matthew 17:20–21 (NIV)

HOW CAN I ENCOURAGE SOMEONE TO GROW IN THEIR FAITH?

Devo - Puzzles - Off to Golf with Chas - Walter Forrest paired 1 - 2 - 5. Not good rest of way. Home to cereal + Sgt. York - Cooper & Teresa Wright - W. Brennan - was Band Great - inspirational movie. Bath + off to Haircut - see Carla - + talk to customers - See end of Here to Eternity - News - Mary & Mark over for supper - Leftovers - see Cagney in Public enemy - + Town without Christmas with Patricia Medina - + Chris (girl) + Colombo as Angel.

Drug bust worth millions in Mpls - Husband a beaten teacher must be nuts -

And this life is eternal, that they might know thee the only true God, and Jesus Christ, whom thou hast sent. —John 17:3

NOVEMBER 28

When did an experience in nature help me to grow close to God?

Devo + Puzzles - Cam to Board Meet - D stretch - walk + lift weights - After lunch go to Stein's & find blood much too thin - Go to Walgreens but they are out of allergy med. - Home - Then to Wild Oats. Ace's. - Fresh market for salmon + choc. blueberries - new girl real friendly. - Get Cam's car gassed. Home with loot. Coffee. Rain all day cancelled golf. - See 1 hr. Moore about Journalist detective - some of Charlie Moran Xmases + 2 "One of Guys" new episodes - School crime on news. Man hired to kill another's wife - no suspect in woman killed then wounded in bed. Bruins - win @ Denver after 17 straight losses - scandal in bugged security office.

NOVEMBER 29

The wisdom from above is first pure, then peaceable, gentle, reasonable, full of mercy and good fruits.... —JAMES 3:17 (NAS)

WHAT OPPORTUNITY CAN I TAKE TO SHARE THE FRUITS OF THE SPIRIT?

Devo - Puzzle -- Balt. off to Underwood to Funeral visitation - Louise Bartley - Then to Episcople Church where we attended Matt Jewell's funeral. Saw "Big Em" - Browns + Whitsetts - Patty has trouble with Roy - From there to Betty with Jewett's luncheon - didn't recognize Martha or Britt's old coach - Chat with Jimmy W/ H.S. daughter. Betty Lyons huffs + puffs through it all - Ride long, slow funeral procession - Graveside ceremony - Matt was Naval Eighter - pilot + Labor negotiator from his U. of Memphis Teaching - Home to Map + News - + cereal supper after the noon feast - Heading for Britt's B.B. game - Ann helps me solve Xm. Puzzle

> "And who knows whether you have not come to the kingdom for just such a time as this?"
> —Esther 4:14 (RSV)

NOVEMBER 30

GOD, HELP ME TO LISTEN FOR YOUR VOICE WHEN I AM STRUGGLING WITH A DECISION.

Devo + USA Puzzle. Ann to Bible Study — I lift weights & we go to 1st E Jan. — Nap — some solitude — Feeb Ford found taking bribes — Former Co. commissioner guilty of Mickey laundering. Lee ugly Betty + later Macey to Ball game — Went for Chicken. Brought Ann home & saw Shark — who's having trouble with daughter — ya hang — Kelly — Mikey + Micah @ game — subs played —

DECEMBER 1

For God so loved the world, that he gave his only begotten Son. . . . —JOHN 3:16

HOW CAN I KEEP MY FOCUS ON LOVE FOR OTHERS THIS HOLIDAY SEASON?

Devo + Puzzle - got 'em both - Go to Comcast for Ann with check - for Cable T.V. - Go get Britt after school - walk - Ann to Dr.'s office - no surgery coming - call for Clay Osen + Mary Company (no ans.) check on air mile requirements -
Watch Being served Papers - see News - Politicians (Mphs) in deep B'room sweep - 4 burglars caught when Truck sticks in muddy lawn. 4 caught slipping drugs - See Phillipine rescue of 'Death March' captives - in prison 3 yrs. See Paratroopers killed + captured by Germans - fought hard.

Then the Lord said to Moses, "I will rain down bread from heaven for you. The people are to go out each day and gather enough for that day...."
—Exodus 16:4 (NIV)

DECEMBER 2

LORD, HELP ME TO SEEK CREATIVE SOLUTIONS TO FINANCIAL CHALLENGES.

Devo - Com. Purr - Read paper reports about councilmen taking bribes -- Money launderer testifies against them - Ann to grocery - I get lotto ticket - & lift weights & stretch - Ga. Tech loses to Wake 9-6 -- Fla. beats Ark. for SEC title - Okla. beats Nebraska - UCLA big upset over S. Cal - who will play in Champ. bowl in Arizona -
Blow leaves in piles - find mower handle broken - but get it started & mulch leaves —— 2 hrs hard work — watch games - Rutgers & W. Va go to 3 overtimes - See Flash repeat. Rape in rec room - daughter fantasizes Bacon & Egg supper.

December 3

Sing unto the Lord a new song. . . .
—Psalm 149:1

Is God encouraging me to try something new?

Up @ 8 - Deco - Puzzle Hot Tebb - off to 1st Edu Home to nap - Vack house + got leaves out of flrd ground up yesterday - very cold 35 - & wind - see news - Jeremy & Kristin over @ 5:30 - Rost for Roast - Kristi uses puter cefter & fern rubber + solo taco - See Eli Manning lose to Titans & Eagles beat Denver - see Without a Trace - girl lies about teacher for scholarship & gets cancer - Mom attacks her. Gets to hospital to see loved ones -

Fla to play Ohio State in Big Bowl - Mich vs. USC in Rose -

> "Store up for yourselves treasures in heaven, where moth and rust do not destroy, and where thieves do not break in and steal."
> —Matthew 6:20 (NIV)

December 4

WHO IN MY LIFE DO I CONSIDER A SAINT ON EARTH?

Puzzle - Devo - Called Clay Isom - Went to David's & got Ann's check - deposited $1100 - To - Mark & Mary over for leftovers - Saw Britt game - to Game stop - got 1 disc -

December 5

> On him we have set our hope that he will continue to deliver us, as you help us by your prayers. . . .
> —II Corinthians 1:10–11 (NIV)

Am I open to the experience of God's healing love?

Devo. Puzzle - Cam to stove - I work in yard - blew mulched leaves in 2 piles & shovel em into cart - blow side - sidewalk - see truck with 911 stickers -

Fall out took Kelly to Covington P. lot & brought him home -

Picked Brill up @ school - yesterday - watched Murder He Says with Marla - + then Close When cop tells informer and fellow cop when he learns he is not the father of son he is caring for -

Lady cop will move in with boyfriend -

News - indicted congressmen & go and vote on issues -

soup for supper -

"And many of those who sleep in the dust of the earth shall awake. . . ." —Daniel 12:2 (RSV)

December 6

Is there a new opportunity that I need to explore?

Most of Puzzle - min EGGO -- Ann to Lindenwood Salvation Army with Betty Witt Jewett - I play golf with Forrest, Walter + Chas - Par 2+3 - double 3 holes - missed putts for 3 Near pars —
Home to cereal + Com Puzzle - Out in yard blowing leaves and lifting them off pool cover - get Michjame halo - 2 potties -
- See Astaire + Hepburn in Funny Face — "Marvelous — one song See ½ of Brits game victory over Cordova - He plays entire game - Well - coached - tease Nancy + Friend — Heckle ump -
Hooks to prison — confesses eight sentence -

December 7

> "Thou liftest me up on the wind, thou makest me ride on it, and thou tossest me about in the roar of the storm." —Job 30:22 (RSV)

How does God comfort me in the storms of my life?

Pearl Harbor Day - Ann to Md Pres - ready for hosting luncheon - I vack house - clean up bed room bath after Ann - dress & go to Sterne's - Kid md floor girls & see Teesha, who is happier upstairs - Get help with puzzle - give candy & PM left good from Faye (Babe) -

Home to meet women then off to 1st Guar. see Kedra & mem - & three new women -

Home to help ladies - down steps - They enjoyed home & decor Ann & I have naps

- See news - & eat ham sand. & salad -

See some 3000 - & Shark - Mom & daughter shoot vellain - more shooting in MPhc. lady cop. hit & run victim

The Lord hath appeared of old unto me, saying, Yea, I have loved thee with an everlasting love. . . .
—Jeremiah 31:3

December 8

How has God shown His love during the transitions in my life?

7 devos - 2 Puzzles - stay home - very cold day. Read from Phillip Keller on 23rd Psalm - 50+ pages - some solitaire - Try to get Bradshaws' - No luck - Ann and I nap - see Numbers - Rudolph & Frosty the Snowman - have Kelly's Potato Soup ½ ham sand - some fruit salad - Make list of To Dos - Don't do any of them - Ann gets dizziness gets over it - I lift weights & stretch

December 9

I will sing of the Lord's great love forever....
—Psalm 89:1 (NIV)

Do I demonstrate my faith in my interactions with others?

Cold day - 2 Dew's - Crsmn Puzzle hard - Mark helps me with cee for circumference - & Eli, st for suit - Go with him to Macy's for suit, I get sport coat - Ann stays & shops & goes to grocery - Mark & I see Ky beat Indiana by 5 points in Lexington. Ga. Tech loses to Vandy - Both look better than Ky.

Mps wins over Ole Miss - Miss State wins - see some Frosty & Rudolph cartoon Lynyrd & Law & Order. Blacks sterilized by Nurse - one dies - found guilty.

I also will requite you this kindness, because ye have done this thing. —II Samuel 2:6

DECEMBER 10

WHEN DID A FRIEND'S KINDNESS ESPECIALLY TOUCH MY LIFE?

Worked puzzle - Missed 2 & 3 letters - Shave & off to 1st Evan. music program. Rowdy little kids in front - Bothered Margie bad + worrisome - Horse to stretch - left weights & walk during Cary & Audree's Charades - Walked Heathrow -- see most of Hannah mystery - about 8 or 9 murders & atomic case explodes - Sam's Chicken supper + picture taking - some of N.O.'s big victory at Dallas - some of closure - Trace start late - Take Hot Tub -

December 11

*I rise before dawn and cry for help;
I hope in thy words.* —Psalm 119:147 (RSV)

AM I WILLING TO ANSWER A CRY FOR HELP AT ANY TIME?

Puzzles - Off to Golf with usual 3 - par par 3 hole - both par 5's - Go to Dr's for chest medicine - Home to cereal - call dentist & Murris, Barnst & Walter -- no golf tomorrow - see news & go to Verett's game - They lose in last 5 seconds - Ref was terrible - ECS win - Home to go see Roberts - + cross street with Nehborhood watch stuff. Eat chicken with Mark & see Mary Poppins & Celtic women -
CSI Miami — two more murders to top last year - Bad dreams last night -

He healeth the broken in heart, and bindeth up their wounds. —Psalm 147:3

DECEMBER 12

IS THERE BROKENNESS THAT I CAN HELP TO REPAIR?

Devo's + 2 Puzzles.
Ann up early to decorate for CWF luncheon — I stretch — left periphls — Hot Tub + to Dentist for inlay glue-on — then for towels for Ann + Dental office — To Church luncheon — + home to nap. Take Ann to deliver Poinsettia to Ruth Edding's Mum — Cat/gets out + finally back in — To Wild Oats for cereal + seed — Home — call Ellis's got tape.
See news + some Raymond after winning Rudolph. Kristin over but can't copy disc — see The Yearling who eats their corn — son runs away + is rescued — Jane Wyman (mum) finally warms up — after losing 3 kids! finds last one at home —
Gregory Peck — Emmet Fard envolved in stealing + selling Church land.
Warm weather tomorrow. Rained over 1 inch last night —

December 13

Do not neglect to do good and to share what you have, for such sacrifices are pleasing to God.
—Hebrews 13:16 (RSV)

With whom will I share my blessings this Christmas? How?

Devo - & puzzle - other on way to exercise. Home to short nap - rack house & get leaves off the sidewalk - see news. Did rubber & some solitaire - Kristie over with pictures - see news & some Raymond - old chicken & potato & receive police lady & cave guests -- Kristens absent & Kaplans Harry here & Dexter (who must have forgotten - Lots of good advice in come & out .. burglary case ave — See love stories on WILND — & Bucket at the castle.
Daddy at police station - Chase agent away — steals part of Richard's car —

A dream cometh through the multitude of business.... —ECCLESIASTES 5:3

DECEMBER 14

HOW CAN I VIEW MY LIFE FROM A DIFFERENT PERSPECTIVE?

Puzzles — Deco — Ann off to shop — No pictures at first — later success — I call David's office — 56,000 coming. Go to 1st Evan... for service — Huffman — Sit by his wife — to Juice Plus — out to Shelby Drive — stop by State Farm for coverage summary — Lift weights + stretch — Mark over for Ugly Betty (gets Emmy nomination) Sgt. York — & I see Shark and Bill Mitchell Court Marshal — Gary Cooper — Ralph Bellamy Rod Steiger —

December 15

Put your hope in God. . . . —Psalm 42:5 (NIV)

IN WHAT SMALL WAY CAN I ENCOURAGE A FRIEND WHOSE FAITH IS CHALLENGED?

Devo - Puzzles - Ann sleeps early - I get leaves off Pool cover. Tough - After cereal lunch blow front yard after nap - Eat spinach soup Kelly made for supper - See Ghost Whisper - Close to home and Numbers - + jet dog fights on History channel - News - Dot d'd to eyes - + bed -

Each of you should look not only to your own interests, but also to the interests of others.
—Philippians 2:4 (NIV)

December 16

HOW MIGHT I SERVE OTHERS MORE IN THESE DAYS BEFORE CHRISTMAS?

Cam, Jazzle + Jevo came to Sam's — Later to grocery + to Bubber's — I sack front yard leaves — mower loses oil cap + starts smoking — can't do back yard — Call Kelly to look @ it but not home — Walk over to see KY/Lousville game — KY wins by 11 — neither team looks good — our 2 stars — one out wrist fouls — didn't help — but Frosh leads + 3's — & leads scorers — wins Top player award — Cocoa's — Get Tiny Migraine — Lift weights & stretch — old beef for supper — see Hitler's casual conversations recreated from silent films — seemed human — didn't like Goering — Eva an athlete out of Public but present at Berchesgarten — See E's famous jeans & some Soap Opera + End of Wonderful Life

December 17

There was no room for them in the inn.
—Luke 2:7

Do I have the opportunity to include new faces in this year's Christmas celebration?

Worked Big puzzle – Did Bike instead of Milk – Hot Tub & 1st Evan – See Ballingers – Home to cereal & nap. Walk 30 minutes in house to music. Harper calls to tell me Harry Wright is dead – Vack a bit – Ann & I fill 2 bags with semi-wet leaves – See some football – Eagles win over Giants & San Diego over Kansas City – see end of Jerry Lee Lewis movie & 2 Being Served shows – Give Jeremy & Kristie presents & get ein from them. Kids enjoy each other – Hug & kiss for Lydia – Hug Nanny & Sue – Mark goes to ailing Marie for her gifts to Jeremy & Kristie. Eat Prime Rib Supper –

Apply thine heart unto instruction, and thine ears to the words of knowledge. —Proverbs 23:12

DECEMBER 18

WHOSE VOICE CAN SOOTHE MY WORRIES?

2 Puzzles - off to exercise - To Kiko - Ann loses keys - finds 'em later in her purse - after we ask everyone in Kinko's if they've seen 'em - To Kinko's - find lady with dead car - $40 for key south - 10 for gas + tip from young man at Shell - - who got gas cap off + poured in one gallon - - Home - nap - do 2 bags of leaves - solitaire - . Mark + Marg. over - see TU. beat Oklahoma State - see Santa 2 - + C S I Miami - Biker in arms deal shoots undercover agent - wife shoot around weapons - abandons wife for work - See Budget at beach restaurant with Romantic European - Sheridan calls for money -

December 19

Therefore let us stop passing judgment on one another. Instead, make up your mind not to put any stumbling block or obstacle in your brother's way. —Romans 14:13 (NIV)

HOW CAN I LIVE MORE POSITIVELY AND FOCUS LESS ON THE MINOR IRRITATIONS OF LIFE?

2 Puzzles - after Devotional - Bathe & Dress for Harry Wright's funeral - Kelly over & fixes our Lawn Mower with 2 new parts - See Flowers - McCrory - Mabry Herrington - Furnest - Kim Falk - Owen Dandos - Walt + Dot - Sam Lewis - Dallas Flowers - Betty & Ken - Kyler - Leave before funeral for Wild Oates - Nap - Shortly - after news - Mark & Mage over - See Kentucky beat Santa Clara - Our center stars — some improvement. see - Without a Trace - Mark leaves - See Closer — Gang killing - wrong victims See Bucket in Ball Costume - Peete & Ford indicted -

Mine eyes are ever toward the Lord. . . .
—Psalm 25:15

December 20

What reminders does God send that His love is unchanging?

Puzzle - off to exercise - Home after lunch @ Charlotte's Ann off for long time - do Rest after wine - Solitaire Coffee - More solitaire + bridge - See News - See B.B. Arkansas - LSU + Washington - 16 pt lead @ half for Washington - See CSI N.Y. - 3 girl Robbers - + African diamond murderer - Cereal for supper with Strawberries + Pineapple - dessert too - Lift Weights

DECEMBER 21

And thou shalt have joy and gladness; and many shall rejoice at his birth. —LUKE 1:14

IN WHAT WAYS DO I SHARE MY JOY AT CHRISTMAS?

Devo - Puzzle - off to Underwood for youth sing and lunch - buy Santo from Dawn Helene & gave it. To Dairy Kidd - & Wild Oats for Marge's Turkey - Home to rest but no nap - got Ann out for short walk - no reading again - see news & Raymond. Mark over for dinner brought home - quite a steal - See some basketball Ohio State beats Pitt - Duke over Gonzaga BYU over Oregon - See Sharks - Producer kills wife and girlfriend - John Ford get $40,000 watch - bribe from developer - Health Care woman steals a million over several years -

In this was manifested the love of God toward us, because that God sent his only begotten Son into the world. . . . —I John 4:9

December 22

WHAT DETAIL OF JESUS' BIRTH IS THE MOST INSPIRING TO ME?

Puzzle — Devo — ?
Too 8:00 Ham pick-up
Black data to Ike's & down
to Lindenwood for
Santa I bought from Pam Heller
Walk with Ann — See Abbie —
Lift weights & stretch — Nap.
When Ruthy & Kelly shred into
presents — So are Bett play well
against Briarcrest — He lost
3 — re Brands & assigly — scores
on full com, & drive (final contest)
home & 300 also & Home & Munk
with pepsy — flex members —

December 23

For unto you is born this day in the city of David a Saviour, which is Christ the Lord. —Luke 2:11

GOD, HELP ME TO FIND A QUIET MOMENT IN WHICH I CAN CONTEMPLATE YOUR GREATEST GIFT.

Puzzle - Devo - House all day. See TU beat Ohio State in O.T. Knight sets new coaching victories at UTEP — Mype. teams every lose — Go to Britt's game — lose by one — Britt steals & scores — misses 2 free throws -- vs. better coached team -- Mark Marg Kelly Nancy all there. Mikey at work — Britt missed 2 free throws — Home to ½ crime series woman pedophile is pregnant — see part of S. Pa Sound of Music and U.S. major under Kamikaze attacks the bomb ends war & saves a million allied casualties. — Rain for Xmas —

The Lord is good unto them that wait. . . .
—LAMENTATIONS 3:25

DECEMBER 24

WHEN DID GOD SEND
BLESSINGS BEYOND MY
EXPECTATIONS?

Devo — Check funnies, + sports and T.V. Guide — Het heb off to 1st Evan. — Sermon on God's coming to earth thru Jesus — Got Asst. Minister — daughter a pew seat — Sit with Mark + Marge — Big crowd — Tell Mark we will cook spaghetti outside — Home to cereal — see end of Kris Kringle + see Titans one pt. win on field goal — vs. Indianapolis + N.Y. Lose badly — Vack rest of house — heading for weightlo. Lift Weights — stretch — see A Christmas Tiny — + much of a Wonderful life — Kids over for spaghetti — No stolley or krispie — Kelly, Marg. + Henry off to Underwood Eve Service — Ann sees most of Xmas Story

DECEMBER 25

And yet I am not alone. . . . —JOHN 16:32

HOW CAN I BLESS SOMEONE WHO IS ALONE TODAY?

Christmas! work puzzle - Mark & Marge over - we open presents - Nancy, Britt & Kelly - presents - late Dinner - Turkey & Ham - Lydia & Mike over for presents & dessert - Dallas loses to Philly Eagles - terrible game. Heat wins over Lakers - see Sam to Claus - and some of Pirates (fighting skeletons?) - girl saves boy - later marries him. Depp gets his Black Pearl back finally - saved from hanging -
James Brown dies - 4 marriages - one jail sentence - S. Carolina arrives for wet Liberty Bowl -
Rains today - -

Praise ye the Lord. Praise God in his sanctuary. . . . —PSALM 150:1

DECEMBER 26

WHEN DID I HAVE A JOYOUS TIME IN UNLIKELY SURROUNDINGS?

Puzzle – Devo – out to 1st TN with Mary & Mark's checks – trouble getting service – had to call Kelly – To Mall after cadence to cash Ruth's $41 check – walked – went to Sears to talk about edger – – didn't buy – To Wild Oats for cereal & stuff – Home – Margie last night stayed & most of day today – Ann calls lads over for supper – get mail – see Dexter & Crested Rice window – Plugs still around – Get Turkey & see Magical Matilda run off Principal – see some who's mine is it (gross) as was Court – – Woman claims to be James Brown's wife – Talk to David about Britt & get clearance – lift weights –

December 27

"Have you comprehended the vast expanses of the earth? Tell me, if you know all this."
—Job 38:18 (NIV)

Is my faith deeper because of the challenges that I've encountered?

Devo & Puzzle - Ann went to Macy's - Took Beth & Lu Lenwood for B.B. Mach's 1½ - Ate cereal - went to P.O. - Ake's - Gas - Margie's Bus to her house - Bridge & Solitair Talked to Ann Bradshaw - Mary Jo Travel Tickets - Cleta Mae - Kay Steed - she's sending me some pills - go in Jan. to get re-instated - See news - eat Turkey - Mary over from shopping - see Lizzie McGuire get famous in Paris - song and dance - See enough of Annie with Finney. Carol Burnette - Fla. State runs over UCLA - Griz 20 lose again - Milwaukee - Rain predicted for late J. Berg month -

May you be blessed by the Lord, the Maker of heaven and earth. —Psalm 115:15 (NIV)

December 28

With what small gesture can I extend a blessing to someone this week?

Puzzles — Ann & to Steve — after walk with Margie — Stretch & lift weights — see Bridge @ Toko-Ri — See some of Gary Cooper's Marco Polo — Sunny show — See Shark repeat — fib in the factory — See Bucket steal Rolls Royce — Eat cereal & salad with Micah — See Ugly Betty — Read some of Phillip Keller on 23rd Psalm — Think of blessings —

DECEMBER 29

Teach me, O Lord, the way of thy statutes; and I shall keep it unto the end. —PSALM 119:33

WHAT DAILY ACTIVITIES CAN I USE TO DEEPEN MY FAITH?

Puzzles - no stretch or walk. Ann off to sleep - Then off to see Mary Jane - lies flat one block away - Gets my car & I get AAA - Gets tire right away. See Ky beat Clemson in Nashville - Clemson favored by 9 - Ky wins by 8 - S. Carolina outlasts Houston in biggest scoring game in Liberty Bowl history - See Center Christ — See Close to Home & move Center Christ — young couple killed in drug murder - See Numbers - drugs & child abuse — See Philippine naval battle - destroyers take on battleships & they turn & run - over 200 US sailors die but protect MacArthur's men on the islands - Halsey tricked & goes north. Mary Jane & Ann go to lunch + come home to visit, she takes her to hotel. Budget Ad leads her to Strip Show & Daddy's There.

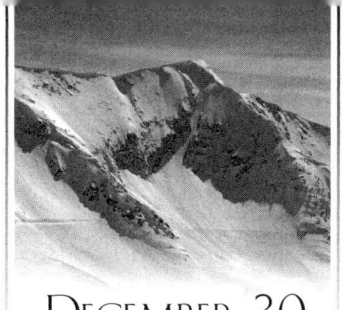

O the depth of the riches both of the wisdom and knowledge of God! . . . —Romans 11:33

DECEMBER 30

DO I HAVE AN OPPORTUNITY TO RELY ON GOD'S WISDOM FOR HELP?

Devo - a old USH's - we later commun. too - ?? weights & stretch - B.C came in 1 sec. field goal over ? - ?? comes back to win over ? after 21 pt. behind - Mary Jane wer for hers talks - take 'em back in review eat lunch + ?? & off to Church for Haley's wedding - don't go to reception - Ruth calls - take first Vess. fruit pills for Ken steed - see Harwoods & Patsy Witt see 2½ ugly Betty's in a row - Being served - med mim selling jobs - can't get fired - Slocum or Gaye -

December 31

I was glad when they said to me, "Let us go into the house of the Lord." —Psalm 122:1 (NKJV)

How will I incorporate worship into my celebration of the new year?

Devo - Com. Puzzle — To 1st Evan. - dozing Baby pitts.. - preacher - check bald heads — Home to cereal & last part a Cerabesque with Tack & Loren - spies lying to each other - Football - Titans lose - Mannings win - see 3 ugly Bettys in a row — & Cinderella Story - Hilary Duff — see some Shark - killer locks Girl in closet during fire - see old Without a Trace - Lesbian girlfriends — see NY eve party & ball come down Dick Clark's had it - slurring words May & Mask over - Spaghetti - Broccoli & lettuce salad —

Jan 1 - 07
Watched football -
  Auburn beats Neb -
  Ga Tech loses - big lead
  TN Loses
  Ark "
  Mich loses to USC
Bad day for me -
  See CSI Miami - serial murders
  - see Monk Twin awful -
  News - Hereafter wants to build new stadium
  - Duan Bronco shot + killed - outside bar
  Kids over for pork supper Ann cooked
  12 lbs - Mike + his dad coming in
  from skiing in W. Virginia -

  Ann + Bubbers with food -

Jan 2 - walked with Ann + Max -
Late breakfast - call David's office +
learn that I can get IRA money. Take
hot bath + shave - To Drucie's with flowers
Back home for undershirts - To Bank -
Pay off loan - + Deposit - - To Witt
Gas + Miss Maria - To Hair cut + meet
Angela + Michael - give an dollar. Grandma
gets out of chair to calm in - my fault
To Alli's - for drugs - home to gym -
see Batman 2 with Mark - Eat
veggies - see some Louisville + Wake
Orange Bowl - see Numbers -
+ News - Ford body sent to Michigan